Our life is limited and we spend more than half of it in employment. Some go beyond that and dedicate much more time to create employment. This book is an attempt to use my life and career for others to refer to, and learn from my successes and mistakes.

This book is dedicated to all entrepreneurs who risked their wealth, dedicated their time and faced all the risks to launch companies, thus providing employment to youth, taxes to the government and products to serve the masses while being alert of their businesses 24 hours a day, 7 days a week.

The Birth

The times were bad enough. Sri Lanka – then Ceylon - was gripped with communal unrest. Chaos was everywhere. Yet there was more to come, as my birth took place during these times (the 1950's) of turmoil, in a southern coastal town of Sri Lanka. I was not born rich, neither was I born poor. Living was easy then and my parents both government employees could afford to bring me up with the little luxuries in life. I wonder what my parents wanted me to grow up as, a doctor, lawyer, engineer or at least a government servant. Only the first three professions were considered in high esteem. But a government employee was thought as someone who was securely employed in those days.

Then how did I end up as an Accountant? This profession was little known during this time and most people thought he is the man standing behind a counter collecting bills. However today with the private sector coming to the forefront the Accountancy profession has enhanced its value and the government employee is less secure of his position with all the privatisations taking place.

Schooling was no hassle. My first education was in a convent (I am a male) later I was in a mixed village school, and in the third year I joined a leading catholic school in Colombo. The change was difficult at first. After being with simple village children suddenly I was in the midst of the spoilt and pampered children of high society. Anyway I was still small enough to fit in.

The first hurdle I had to clear was the new English oriented education of the school. Unlike today most of the students spoke English, read many English books, as television was just a lesson in the science book. Memories of school days are pleasant. In the first year we had an English lady who thought us almost all the subjects. She was a stern disciplinarian with short crop hair and court shoes, a novelty in those days. She brought us shivers when she walked the corridors. School days were just school days, those were the days I still look back with envy. I experienced what any ordinary boy would during his school days and the pleasant memories were just the same. There was one genius of a student who used to get the first prize in all subjects from year 3 till he left school. He deprived me of getting a prize in at least my 2 favourite subjects – Sinhala and English Languages. He used to read 'Das Capital' in year 7. I see him nowadays on TV political programmes, as he has ended up as a political critic.

In those bad old days our school was considered the best in Sri Lanka. We also had one of the best swimming pools in Asia – during these times the second largest bookshop in the world was also in Sri Lanka. We had the best cricket record in Sri Lanka and many more plus points. The hierarchy of the school consisted mainly of priests and thus strict discipline prevailed. The total moulding of the individual was enough for even the dumbest nut to at least end up as a security supervisor. Running a school of this nature was not easy. Our school fell into the category of assisted schools. They got no help from the government and were prohibited from levying fees from the students. How this situation came to being is a long story, which I am compelled to write here.

Long ago Sri Lanka had many types of schools. Most of the schools like the one I went to took the form of a private institution imparting education for a fee. It was the societies' affluent people who were able to reap the benefit of this education. The poor village boy had the ill equipped village school to learn to read and write, but many sages and viziers had started their education in these schools. Then one politician brought the concept of "Free Education" and made sure that government schools will not charge a red cent from the students. As for the private schools he offered to give them grants for their expenses. Some private schools rejected this offer and preferred to continue as private institutions levying fees from students. But most of them including my school, took advantage of this and became "Assisted Schools".

Things has been quite all right until in the 1960's when the then government thought that they should not help private schools from public funds. As such they wanted to nationalise all private schools. Knowing the clear difference between the government and private schools, the people strongly objected going to the extent of processions and protests. After finally giving in to this resistance the government cancelled its decision to nationalise schools. Anyway the assisted schools were denied any grants from the government – and they were prohibited from levying fees from students. This went on fine as the private schools stopped charging fees but collected donations, which were mandatory, but not illegal. Though students could refrain from contributing these fixed monthly donations the prestigious environment of most schools compelled them to give their donations as otherwise he would be a misfit among other students. There were also many schools, which could not carry on like this and had to ultimately hand over the schools to the government. But our school though sometimes it had problems paying its bills, stands as strong as ever even today.

In the last years of my school days which were the late 70's my father bought me a moped, probably the cheapest model in the world and I was the first student to go to school in a motorised vehicle in its entire history. I also got an electronic calculator as a gift from my uncle that I would carry and show to everyone with such pride.

I always considered myself as a "would be scientist". I enjoyed repairing broken toys and gadgets. When my uncle qualified as a Chartered Accountant I did not take it seriously, though he received a salary of about 5 times that of my Father. He even had a car, a luxury that only a few people enjoyed those days. The road was all yours at that time. School days kept going very slowly and in the last years of school I was very weak in Chemistry. The subject was very much necessary to be a Doctor or Engineer. My childhood dream was to become a pilot. I was fascinated by the aeroplane, but the facility to become a pilot was not available so easily unless you joined the air force. There were two small practice planes in Sri Lanka and those who wish to become a pilot had to wait long to get a turn to fly these. Unfortunately on of these planes hit a coconut tree and then there was only one left. So I had to wake up from my childhood dream. However when my uncle advised me on the merits of doing Accountancy I thought I should give it a try.

It was always desirable for someone pursuing a career in Accountancy to work in an audit firm. These firms while doing a critical examination of records of a variety of organisations, also gives valuable training to those employed by them as trainees. In view of this my father took me to Williams and Company through the influence of my uncle to put me on my first job. Having a son in employment just after leaving school was supposed to be a great relief for my father.

When we met Mr.Herat, a partner of the company my father was very keen on seeing me employed as a trainee. However Mr.Herat advised me to first pass in four advanced level subjects before joining his firm. His main argument was that once I am employed with new responsibilities and activities I may not be able to fulfil the basic requirement to register as a student in the Chartered Institute. This was of course very valuable and timely advice, which influenced the course of my life. Knowing my limitations I took a quick course to learn Logic and Accounts. Logic was easy dealing with an if-then relationship. The most common, which I still have in memory, is "If all men are mortal and Aristotle is a man, therefore Aristotle is mortal." Another riddle associated with the subject was "If the barber in London shaves only the beard of everyone who does not shave their own beard, does he shave his own beard?" If you are not familiar to Logic you will notice that this question cannot be answered Yes or No. Both answers will be subject to argument. For example if we answer "yes", that means the barber shaves his own beard. But the barber will not shave the beard of such people according to the statement. Therefore the answer can be deemed wrong. On the other hand if we answer "no" that means the barber is a person who does not shave his own beard. But the statement clearly says that the barber will shave the beard of everyone who does not shave his own beard. Therefore even the answer "no" is wrong.

Another riddle associated with Logic was also interesting. It is where a king sentences a man to death. Before putting him to death the king grants him an opportunity to make a last statement to the public. Based on whether the statement is True or False the king will put the man to death respectively by hanging or burning. The man taking this opportunity makes the statement thus: "The king will now put me to death by burning". This leads to confusion, for if the king puts him to death by burning the man's statement becomes true. The king has assured that if the statement is true the man will be put to death by hanging. Similarly if the king puts him to death by hanging the man's statement becomes false and the king has promised to put him to death by burning if the statement is false. Ultimately the king had no option but to let the man go free.

Though Logic was fun Accounts was a serious subject. Being used to science for over fifteen years the sudden transition was not easy. Here I was totally confused with words like debit and credit and other jargon. However it did not take long for me to grasp the roots of the whole thing. Though many rules and methods of memorizing were there I remembered the terms debit and credit in the following manner. If we have a cash box we will fill it with what we receive. These are the debits to the cashbook, which will be written on the left half of a paper divided into two with a vertical line in the middle. Similarly things that reduce the amount in the cash box are written on the right hand side. Of course you may now have realised that the difference in the totals in either side represents the balance in the cash box. As cash cannot take a negative value always the left half of the paper should be more. As we know on which side of the cash book a transaction is written we can now come to the conclusion that the other entry goes to some other account and to the opposite side than that of the cash book. Thus if we buy a car, we debit Motor Car account and credit the Cash Book. If we sell goods we credit Sales account and debit the Cash Book. Now that we are dead sure of the sides to which our double entry is recorded we can figure out what will happen if these transactions take place on credit without any cash getting involved. Of course the side that we decided earlier in relation to a cash transaction cannot change. So the entries will be something like Motor Car account debit and Toyota Co. Ltd. Credit and Trade Debtors account debit and Sales account credit. If this has given you some pain of mind please note that others in my class took a greater effort to learn the double entry rule, memorising many rules and yet not grasping it properly.

After a few months of tuition I had a good hold on the subject of accountancy and was now even coaching others on the subject. When someone new to accounts is confused as to what a Balance Sheet and Profit & Loss account is, I had a favourite and simple example, which was designed by me and is stated here for your information.

A father who wants to give his daughter in marriage has three suitors in line. Being quite business minded the question he puts forward to the suitors is how much are they worth? Value here depends on material wealth only. As the answer to this lets say the suitors give there worth as follows. The currency type is rupees, which is what is used here in Sri Lanka.

A – Rs.1,000,000

B – Rs. 100,000

C – Rs. (100,000)

Please note that C is not worth anything as he is having a negative or minus value. Now who is the best person to be the future partner of the daughter? It should be A of course who is worth a million. Poor C the beggar not worth anything but just a liability. Now we will call the value of these people by a word called 'Capital'. Will the man give the daughter to A who is worth a million. The man will not. Rather than being satisfied with numbers he will want to know what the capital is represented by or what these numbers consist of. Once we analyse this situation we will discover the following.

A

Brand New Motor	3,000,000
Less: Bank loan	2,000,000
Rs.1,000,000	

B

Motor Cycle	50,000
Cash in Hand	50,000
Rs.100,000	

C

Supermarket in Town	700,000
Less: Loan balance	800,000
Rs.(100,000)	

Now to whom would you give your daughter in marriage? Would you like to have A for a son in law? With his brand new car he would have impressed you already. But can he feed your daughter, maintain his car and pay off the bank loan at the same time. Well B might be better with no worries in his head a simple man with some money in his hand and if your daughter looks sweet upon a seat of a motorcycle made for two B can be considered. Then what about C with great earning potential from his supermarket he will of course pay off the remaining loan in no time and at this stage anyone will be influenced to give his daughter in marriage to C.

Well, now we have given the Balance Sheets of A, B and C. above. And the Balance Sheet reveals how much a person is worth. Yet our man is not satisfied. He wants to know how the three suitors reached this stage in their life. So he just wants to know how from the past year they developed into what they are worth today. This is what it revealed.

A

Motor Car	3,000,000
Less: Loan	2,100.000
	Rs.900,000

B

Bicycle	5,000
Less:Bank Loan	250,000
	Rs.(245,000)

C

Supermarket	700,000
Less:Bank Loan	500,000
	Rs.200,000

I think what we now know is enough to make a final decision. C has during the year rather than accumulating profits, taken bank loans to keep his business going. Thus he has reduced himself to a minus value from a better stage a year earlier. A is better than C. he has been earning something to pay at least Rs.100,000 from his loan. But look at B who has risen from rags to riches. Starting off just one year ago with a bicycle and a loan to pay, he has not only paid off the loan and saved some extra money, but has also replaced his old bicycle with a motor cycle of some prestige. I recommend B without fear, will you?

What a person did to change his value during this one year is shown clearly in a profit and loss account, and together with the balance sheet they form the financial reports valued by any business. With similar examples like this I simplified what I have to learn and what I had to teach others.

Though done with haste I got my passes in Accounts, Logic, Pure Maths and Physics – four subjects from different categories – a real fruit salad.

Then one year later when I met Mr.Herat I was totally welcomed to his establishment. The first days in office was a real torture as I was a very shy person by nature taking a long time to adapt to a new environment, but the situation was eased as most of my colleagues were from the same school that I studied in. I was also working under some young well- qualified chaps, who were the perfect role models I wanted to be one day.

The world of the employed

Here I was in employment straight after school. Williams & Company is a firm of chartered accountants, the two partners of the firm being Mr.Williams and Mr.Herat. After joining this firm I came to know that Mr.Williams too studied in the same school as I did and that his son, who was also my classmate worked in the same office. The designation of anyone who joined the firm as an amateur is 'Audit Trainee' and was paid something like the equivalent of 10 US dollars at that time during the late 70's. The people were all dynamic and fun loving, and the work environment was very pleasant.

The very first audit that I went to was that of a large government corporation. The government during this era had imposed strict restrictions on imports and corporations and other state owned institutions reigned in the trade sector. The audit was one taking nearly six months and the team included some dynamic and qualified people. The corporation was far from the capital and travelling a few kilometres was fun. In fact auditing was more or less like being in the campus while getting some pocket money. There were many new words that I had not heard before. For instance adding up some numbers was called 'casting'. Different accounts were bound together in a book called the 'ledger'. The pages of this ledger book were 'folios'. So the very first day I could come home and tell my parents that I did a lot of casting of ledger folios. Isn't it quite impressive?

Auditors were considered of high esteem. They were in one way a nuisance to everyone, prying into records until some discrepancy could be found. On the other hand they brought fear to many as they would spot their errors or omissions and report it to the board of directors. The young audit clerks just entering into the profession were pursuing a career that will place them in the high-income segment of society in the near future. Though many enter and only few survive, no one knew which, and therefore every audit clerk had some appeal as a future executive. Girls did not hesitate to get as close to them as possible to catch them before it was too late.

Casting of ledger folios had to be done manually. However when the volume is large we used adding machines that were more like slot machines. You had to press buttons and pull the handle to do the additions. Well, it was not the Stone Age; some adding machines were using electricity. In my first experience with the adding machine I thought I must find a way to use it in a more convenient manner. If I could remember the way the number keys are placed I could use it while I am looking away. This was not difficult for me as I was already good at typing. Just like in a telephone the number five was in the centre. Placing my middle finger on the '5' key I keyed in numbers slowly but accurately and totally by memory. I mastered the adding machine so quickly that passers-by stopped to watch me use it.

As external auditors we had to work in offices of many clients. Our company was doing the audits and some other services like bookkeeping, tax work etc. for most clients. The type of clients ranged from sole proprietorships to multi-national organisations. There were tea estates, hotels, distilleries, architects, doctors, engineers and many more. Though I was thorough with accounts academically I was now practically involved in using it. Figures were no longer amounts in a test paper. They were money belonging to businessmen whose foundation depended on it. We would go to clients' offices, check their records for accuracy etc. and prepare the Profit and Loss account and Balance Sheet for them. After that we would bring it to the partners of Williams and Company, either to Mr.Williams or Mr.Herat. Most of my work were supervised by Mr.Herat. I was fascinated by the way he would look at a final account and tell what is going on in a business. It could be theft or pilferage. He would see it through the set of accounts. Later I realised some points that made it possible to interpret accounts and get a picture of what is going on in a business. For instance if a retailer has a profit margin of 10% on his purchases, his gross profit has to be 10% of purchases. If it drops to something like 5% that means that someone has stolen half the goods.

I worked as a junior accounts clerk for just a little over three months and after that I was handling audits all by myself, with newcomers working under me. I was still just awaiting my advanced level results. As I still did not have the necessary qualifications register with either the institute of Chartered Accountant, or Management Accountants I was still feeling uneasy about what the future is going to be. However when the results came and I was suitable do the chartered exams it was a great relief.

Suddenly I realised that I was no more the little guy who was pursuing a career in accountancy. I was somebody. I clearly felt the changes in attitudes and the way everyone looked at me. I had the prestige of saying that I was a chartered student. The most popular accounting bodies in Sri Lanka were the Institute of Chartered Accountant of Sri Lanka, and the Institute of Cost and Management Accountants. The former being entirely a Sri Lankan affair was inexpensive to the students. The latter being a London based institution cost about ten times more as the Sri Lankan rupee was far less in value compared to the Sterling Pound. Accountants who completed all exams of these institutions were called Chartered Accountants and Cost Accountants respectively. There was a bigger demand for chartered accountants and they were paid higher salaries in Sri Lanka. Also the main purpose in working in an audit firm for a small allowance was to obtain the compulsory training for chartered examinations. Therefore I got registered in the Institute of Chartered Accounts for Sri Lanka. The next step was to join an institution that conducts classes in accountancy, and there were many choices in Sri Lanka. They were so popular that even foreign students used to attend these classes.

The first day in class was thrilling. It was a "one small step for a day, but a giant leap for the future" with apologies to Neil Armstrong. I still can recite like a parrot the very first paragraph which I learnt in relation to auditing: "An audit is such a critical examination of books accounts and supporting documents, so as to enable a person so examining to express his independent professional opinion on the accounts and statements he has been called upon to report on either by statute or under a private agreement." The lectures were conducted in the premises of St.Peter's College, which was a branch of my own school about half a century back. The rector of the college also happened to be the vice principal of my school when I was in my advanced level classes. As such walking into the rooms of this school was quite nostalgic.

The office environment was fun. More than the fun the urge to absorb as much as possible from this environment was very strong. This was where my foundation is being formed to be what I am going to be in the future. Computers were a luxury during these times. So we were using brains to download everything.

Talking about our office I must describe my bosses Mr.Williams and Mr.Herat. The audit clerks were mainly dealing with Mr.Herat who was in charge of most of the audits of various companies. Mr.Williams on the other hand was dealing with tax matters and spent very little time with the audit clerks. Being much senior than Mr.Herat he also was strict with the staff, but was a jolly good fellow. One thing he was famous for were the long sessions of advice and instructions he used to give to the audit clerks who get trapped into these sessions. Though long and boring it takes years to realise that all his words come into practical use at some stage in your career. He was always at the commanding end, and did not tolerate opposition. When a clerk cuts into his speech session he would strongly command, "now you listen to me first", but that second chance would never come. He was fun loving and encouraged recreational activities and sports. He hated anyone who did not attend to office parties or trips. I can remember one humorous incident involving such an advice session that took place during his time.

During these times, which were the early 1980's there was one form of gambling that was very famous in Sri Lanka. That was horse racing. Though races were not held in the country, Sri Lankans placed their bets on horses that raced in England through agents who were referred to as "bookies". Our office peon (one who runs errands for everyone and does odd jobs) would bring the racing news and we would choose our horses and give him the chits with money. The next day he would bring the results along with the cash winnings of the lucky ones. None of us were severely addicted to this, but most of us were doing this for the fun of it. Though fun for us this type of gambling was a major social problem in Sri Lanka, bringing misery and misfortune to many families. It was an activity looked upon with scorn by everybody. One day our Mr.Williams had given one clerk named Amila, some work relating to the tracing of an error in a large account. After tracing the error he had happily gone to Mr.Williams with the documents to show him where the mistake was. When Amila sat down in front of Mr.Williams the question asked from Amila was "Do you race?" as Mr.Williams had wanted to know whether Amila was also involved in gambling. Unfortunately Amila thought the question was "Did you trace?" and having traced the mistake in the account happily said "yes". Next, a one hour session of advice followed on the evils of gambling. After listing to this one hour lecture Amila replied that he does not gamble but mistook Mr.Williams question to one regarding the mistake that Amila traced. Mr.Willams was furious for the one hour of his time that was wasted and a half an hour of scolding followed.

The examinations of the Institute of Chartered Accountant of Sri Lanka consisted of four stages. The Intermediate level, that consisted of two stages namely preliminary and licentiate and the Final level that consisted of two stages called Associate I and II. It was compulsory for one who completes the Licentiate stage to prove practical training in an audit firm. It was only then that he gets a Licentiate certificate that gives him the prestige of being a half-baked accountant. I too after trotting to classes for nearly six months sat for the preliminary examination. I had a lot of confidence of coming out with flying colours as the papers were easy and as I had a background in both mathematics and accounts, that was a great advantage. Waiting for the preliminary results made things a bit boring, as until the results came classes for the next stage will not commence. So I decided to start doing the examinations of the Chartered Institute of Management Accountants also. These examinations consisted of five stages, the foundation level consisting of stage A & B, and the Professional level consisting of Part I, II and III. One had the options of doing both A and B of the foundation stage in one sitting though one rarely dared to. But getting a kick out of challenges I decided to do both together. More examinations meant more classes and lectures. A major part of my weekend was now dedicated for my career. All my other interests were suddenly being over shadowed. I was fond of writing stories and poetry. But suddenly it came to a standstill. I anyway managed to continue my Karate classes to maintain the balance between my mental and physical activities.

I was still using my moped to come to work most of the time. Though like a push cycle girls would often beg for a ride when we go to conduct audits in other companies. The moped was definitely not meant for two, but in Sri Lanka a bus meant for 30 passengers will generally carry 130. So it was with me. However now that I am employed the desire to buy a motorcycle was deeply in me. The cost of a motorcycle was approximately 120 times my salary. But why can't I collect money and buy one. It will not take more than ten years if I keep collecting my salary. So I started on my long-term plan to collect every penny to buy a motorcycle. However during the first month my father found employment in Saudi Arabia, where the salaries were about five times that of Sri Lanka and promised to send me money to fulfil my ambition. Since then my heart was beating to the rhythm of the motorcycle's beat. I was now visiting motorcycle sales and one model took my fancy. The Bus service was still poor and with the sudden boom in the economy the same number of buses had to carry more passengers to work.

Now with the ideal motorcycle in my mind I was waiting for the money. After about two months my father sent me a bank draft sufficient to buy the motorcycle of my choice. Obtaining money for a draft was not easy. It was not the Internet age. Once the draft was deposited you had to wait until the bank could obtain approval by mail or by telegraph for a fee. Therefore I was a regular visitor to the bank to see whether the balance in my savings account had increased. Even if the money came to the account I had to give a letter requesting to withdraw the money after one week. However when I one day found that the money had been credited to the account, I prepared the letter requesting permission to withdraw it in one week. But fortunately or unfortunately I met one of my friends working in the bank and he gave his authority to withdraw the cash immediately. Since my heart was still beating to the tune of the motorcycle engine, I immediately went to the motorcycle sale to buy my model. After paying the money and buying it now I had to come home. But this was the very first time I had motorcycle in my hand. Although my moped was motorised the concept of the clutch and gears was quite new to me. But I got a few tips from the salesmen and managed to bring the thing home mostly on first gear.

On the same day at mid night the government issued a gazette notification waiving government duties and taxes that amounted to about 50% of the value of a motorcycle. This brought down the prices of motorcycles by one third. My motorcycle which I bought for Rs.15950 was now Rs.11300 and available in wayside showcases. Not being satisfied with simply bringing down the prices the government liberalised loan policies for those who wanted to buy motorcycles and in no time it became the common man's mode of transport.

Whatever it is, the motorcycle made it easier for me to attend lectures as sometimes the evening classes were conducted in a different locations. During these days the results of the first examination were released and as I thought, I had passed. With the new development I had to study also for the second examination of the Institute of Chartered Accountants of Sri Lanka while doing the first two examinations of the Chartered Institute of Management Accountants. So the motorcycle came in very handy to attend lectures here and there. It was also a handy vehicle for the ladies in office to do their errands during the lunch hour, as public transport was still in a chaotic state. So without hesitation I always saw to their needs whether in office or in a client's office, though it was the envy of everyone else.

Here I was preparing at the same time for three examinations. Many advised me against doing so as it was supposed to be too much for the mind. However I found the subjects interesting and could handle many questions by common sense, and when the results came I had passed both the exams of the Chartered Institute of Management Accountants together. I was among 120 such students in the whole world and in Sri Lanka including myself there were 4 students who passed both these exams together. It was time to celebrate. I felt like being a celebrity. However later in my life I thought that this was one of the mistakes I had made in my life. The feeling of pride I had at this time is more or less like the temporary kick one gets after a few tots of alcohol.

There were many reasons behind my success in these first exams. I was addicted to reading. A good part of the pennies I received will go for books. The library was my regular oasis. I was also interested in knowing all types of subjects be it science or astrology. I also did not miss many of the international newsmagazines and monthly digests. Since accountancy was a very practical subject and dealt with your environment I already had acquired the knowledge to face the first examinations. Though many took this rapid progress as a superior skill, unfortunately it was not. The fact that it was not took so long to discover, as even today after over 30 years I have not got through my final examination.

Fun with numbers

This book is written mainly to concentrate on the incidents and challenges one may have to face in pursuing a professional career. However I find it so difficult to distinguish between what is relevant and what is not. I was at Williams & Company for seven years and whatever happened here would have had a lasting impact on me. This is the place where accountants are created, moulded and made. At the time of joining we were not supposed to use calculators, and were encouraged to do our calculations by memory. It was I who started the tradition of depending more on the calculator going to the extent of persuading the company to pay for the batteries.

We had many interesting people in the company. Everyone was fun loving and jovial. So whatever incidents took place were sweet memories rather than horrible ones. We were the inter auditors carom champions in Sri Lanka. We had players who would pot all 9 dogs on the board in his first chance of play without giving the opponent even a chance to play. Our recreation time was mainly round the carom board, some playing some cheering. It was during these sessions that one girl seemed to insist on having me as the partner in playing doubles.

I was never a romantic guy, and was never good at approaching girls. If it is difficult to understand there is a joke about this guy who was just like me. At a party where the majority were ladies he asked his friend how he should start a conversation with a lady. His friend gave a simple instruction: "Just talk something simple. For instance ask her whether she is married, and after that ask her how many children she has." Keeping these instructions in mind he approached a lady and nervously asked how many children she has. When the lady said she has four children he asked her whether she is married. What the results would have been I need not write.

I also cannot alienate myself from writing a few things about the few love affairs that cropped up in the office. All these happened to people who were pursuing a professional career. All these affairs would have acted as some sort of a constraint or catalyst in their careers. I have a feeling that my affair was the most hilarious if not the most disastrous. When a girl was very keen on playing doubles with me and being dropped home in my car, I did not take it so seriously. But instinct was taking priority and I found myself being drawn like a magnet towards her. Then without a warning we ended up as lovers. Here I was getting my first taste of romance and gradually I was getting a taste of the bitter core of the sugar coated pill. We would always go places, the day would start beautifully and towards evening it was war. How things could turn out in such a manner was not logical. It would be a simple statement like, "I see you are having a nice brown purse", for which there will be a counter statement like "Is it only now that you noticed my purse" and it would be arguments, cursing and weeping after that. Things went on like this and in ten months it broke up for good. I felt like someone just out of prison after the break up.

Most of my colleagues who had similar experience ended up tying the knot. The demand for budding accountants was such many girls gave up their boyfriends for good in order to venture into the professional world by marrying an accountant. One interesting case was one which happened to my friend Sugath. Having qualified and after joining another company as accountant, he was approached by a sweet little girl for basic accounting lessons. He did not think much but willingly helped her as she had a steady boyfriend from her school days. However lessons developed into going in the same bus, and she was gradually avoiding going home with her boyfriend on his motor bike. Things were developing fast and one day her boyfriend slapped her while she was having a chat with Sugath at the bus stand. This was embarrassing for both the girl and Sugath, as at this point their love for each other were flourishing. The next day however the girl's former boyfriend met Sugath and apologised for his behaviour and has told Sugath that if he keeps meeting her often he must marry her. A show of sincere love for his childhood sweetheart. Though Sugath did not make a commitment at this point today he is married to this girl and has been living happily ever after.

One of my school mates by the name of Charles also joined the company as an accounts trainee. Being brought up in a closed environment by strict parents it was like the pigeon out of the cage for him. First he took to smoking heavily. A proof of manliness that he tried in vain to portray. Not stopping at that he also tried to show his skill in drinking alcohol straight from the bottle without mixing with anything. His next step was to make a pass at a fair maiden who worked with us in this same office. Though Charles was moving towards disaster he was popular, and decent and there was no reason for any girl to reject him. Anyway he was still not showing any signs of total deterioration. So the girl, Nikki was her name, though keeping a safe distance encouraged him to get to know her more by visiting her home as a friend.

Nikki was not qualified and was not pursuing any professional career. She was religious and calm. She was also sweet and beautiful and was made of sugar and spice and all the things nice. Though she was working with us as being at home may be boring her one ambition in life was to become a good wife and a mother as soon as possible. So Charles' intentions on her was fair and natural. I would not have mentioned yet that by this time my father had sent me money to buy a car and I had one to get about. It was dubbed the "Jingle Bells" for the music coming from its reverse horn. It was also popular with the girls as they found it both fun and safe to move around with me. So sweet Nikki was also a regular passenger in my car. One day I dropped into one of our client's offices while giving her a lift to a fashion store. When I visited the clients office she too got down from the car and came along with me as she was young and discovering the world and was bored of staying seated inside the car. When I was talking with the accountant of that company she had followed up the stairs and by a twist of fate, she met that accountant and just exchanged a few words. After that many telephone calls were exchanged and it turned into romance, and plans for a wedding were on the way.

Charles was furious. Losing complete control over himself he ended up in the lunatic asylum and has not been in his senses since then. Nikki is of course happy and has got a good husband and wonderful in laws, rather than heading into disaster with Charles. I think as a female Nikki had more intelligence than a qualified person. Though she was not with the books she knew the real art of decision making which we accountants try our best to master. Decision making is choosing between alternatives. Sometimes the results whether favourable or adverse takes long to materialise. It is not unusual to see educated, qualified people living a hazardous life due to the lack of knowledge in facing life's day to day challenges. Some give in to their instincts or urges little realising that it is not as rewarding as looking ahead of the horizon and planning methodically before stepping forward. It is very clear that Nikki had made the right decisions, chosen the proper alternative and planned for the future well in advance.

We had many interesting people in this company, some for their weaknesses and some because they simply loved to laugh and entertain others to a good laugh. Tony was a person I should write about. First of all I cannot remember how Tony ended up working with us. Did I say working? Tony was a mischievous delinquent whose sister being a qualified accountant could manage to get Tony employed in Williams & Company. Tony hated work. He had a special talent. That is if he was given a list of ten numbers to be added, he could keep the pen to the first number and like a statue wait for even three or four hours without doing anything, something that will drive any other person nuts. He never thought of making use of his surrounding to get somewhere in the professional world. Therefore everyone avoided taking him as an assistant when carrying out audits. I had some ability to get the most out of people. So anyone considered a misfit always ended up being my subordinate. It was not unusual to hand over to me assignments thought to be impossible along with subordinates who were also thought to be impossible.

So for one fine audit where we had to travel a long distance, we took Tony along. The audit was that of a tea estate far away from Colombo, the capital of Sri Lanka. On such audits the audit clerks had to stay in a guesthouse for a few days and carry out the audit. The audit was in the hands of Kevin who was the senior clerk in charge of it. Though I was a senior too for these prestigious audits, we went even as a subordinate just for the thrill of it. Though the trip was a long way I decided to come in my car. I was not paid for fuel but the bus fare of all of us put together was sufficient to foot the bill. On the first day we decided to start early to enjoy the sceneries and beaches that were in plenty on the way. But alas! Tony came late and upset all our plans. At this time though I was against mistreating anybody I thought that we must give him a punishment when we reach our destination. Whatever the constraints we still managed to enjoy our trip, occasionally following another vehicle if there was a beautiful girl in it, and finally reached our destination.

We first went to a guesthouse where we would later be greeted by the manager of the tea factory. The guesthouse was situated on top of a small hill, surrounded all round by neatly grown lines of tea bushes. As the area was much above sea level the climate was comfortably cool, giving an impression of outdoor air conditioning. The guesthouse was also equipped with a traditional cook who could turn stones into edible pudding. The stay was enjoyable and memorable. Later, we were met by officials of the factory and we made it a point to visit areas in the town in my car. Some hills were so steep that you had a fear of slipping back if the car engine stops by any chance. After a few days of work we decided to activate my resolution to give some sort of punishment (or rag according to campus terminology) to Tony for being such a miserable person. One day in the morning Tony woke up and was about to come out to the garden. But feeling lazy and unfit he went back to bed to get 40 winks. Kevin was of course fast asleep. I and Sarath thought that our patience is much misused, yet we carried on. Therefore we planned to leave a plastic bucket on top of the door so it will fall on Tony when he gets up and comes out into the garden. We then came to the garden and taking a hosepipe started washing my car. After a little while Kevin came to us and grabbing the hosepipe started squirting us with water. Of course this was revenge for the bucket of water had fallen on him. Lucky Tony who was about to come to the garden has fallen asleep and Kevin who was in deep slumber had woken up. So our prank meant for Tony had misfired.

We did not give up. Our next plan was to shave off half of Tony's moustache. So in the evening we prepared a disposable razor and soap, but the next problem was to hold Tony so that we can carry out our treacherous plan. First we decided that I will hold Tony's legs and either Kevin or Sarath will hold his arms while the other shaves Tony's moustache. I being a karate black belter knew a few knots and grips that could pin down a person for a while. Unfortunately, the others though maybe stronger than me could not hold Tony's arm effectively while I was holding his legs. Tony's legs were immovable but he waved his arms around violently while Kevin and Sarath was holding on to them. Then I took charge of his arms and Kevin and Sarath held the two legs. Again it was chaos, as Tony's arms were now firmly locked he bent and straightened his legs violently, along with Kevin and Sarath who were holding them which gave the appearance that they were on a joy ride in an amusement park. The next step was obvious. We had to give up face to face combat and resort to guerrilla tactics. So we decided to wait until Tony fell asleep.

Sarath woke me up close to midnight, but our effort to wake up Kevin failed. Anyway as Tony was asleep Sarath and I decided to carry out our plan by ourselves. So we prepared the razor, soap and brush to clean shave half of Tony's moustache. First we had to trim the moustache with a pair of scissors. So we started clipping away Tony's moustache little by little. After a good part of it was trimmed Tony woke up. We saw anger in his face but what had happened had happened. Then what about the soap and razor and water which we had painstakingly prepared for the occasion? Since accountancy deals with making maximum use of limited resources we decided to use it on Kevin who was fast asleep. Kevin was fast asleep while we trimmed, applied the soap and shaved half his moustache. He woke up when everything was over. As he woke up his stern question was, "What the hell are you doing Joe?" to which my obvious answer was. "We were shaving half of your moustache". His next question was "Why the hell are you doing this Joe?" for which I did not have an answer, and as if sitting for a very tough examination I was dumbfounded. Kevin reacted violently. Since violence towards humans is unethical he took the razor and angrily broke it into two. Then he went outside and threw it far down the hill so that its memory would be lost for ever. However I managed to go down the hill and find it and keep it for a long time as a souvenir. Tony and Kevin of course had to shave their half shaved moustaches completely.

As Tony managed to escape all the onslaughts, and poor innocent Kevin took the beating we tried one last resort of punishment by applying chilli powder in Tony's underwear. Tony wore the underwear on our way back but he did not notice or feel it and we thought that God always helps the damned.

The desire of anyone doing his advanced level examination is to come out with flying colours and to enter the University. However people like me who cannot meet that requirement find other avenues for the journey of life. Naturally it is the real intellectuals who enter the university. But what is the best choice. Once we played a cricket match with the Kelaniya university team. Of course cricket is fun and the spectators have their share of shouting cheering and jeering. When the cheering, jeering and shouting reached a high crescendo, the university students shouted that audit clerks have not even completed elementary school. Our jeer was thought provoking. We shouted back that once they go through years of turmoil we will be part of the board of directors interviewing them for jobs. The jeer and counter jeer ended there. This was of course very much true, and is what happens in most of the cases. For instance if someone jumps school in grade eight and joins a hotel to wash plates, once his friend takes another four years in school and six years in the campus, the one who started first would have come a long way and by now could be a manager of the hotel drawing a comfortable salary. The person who comes out of the campus will have to start finding employment, and will be in square one when his friend has almost reached the summit.

Office career was very much progressive. My salary sort of doubled every year during my seven year period at Williams and Company. It was during the first six years something like Rs. 125, 250, 450, 900, 1500, 2250 which means the salary had kept almost doubling. The initial progress that I made in my professional examinations were such that today I am nowhere near the goal which everyone imagined I will end up one day.

The career at Williams and company started with the end of the 70's and Sri Lanka was changing rapidly. By the time that we entered into the eighties, Sri Lanka was changing very fast due to liberalisation of the economy. With almost everyone trying to make money from the new opportunities, the concept of public companies and share issues was beginning to crop up. A popular bank put its shares to the public. With my father abroad and getting pocket money from him I too bought 100 shares just to improve my knowledge in the accountancy field. After that many companies followed suit, and I did not hesitate to get down their prospectuses to invest in 100 shares being the minimum one is allowed to acquire. 100 shares cost Rs.1000/- in Sri Lankan currency.

One fine day a call came to Williams and Company and as I was near the phone I answered it. A lady spoke from the other end wanted to talk to one of our partners or superiors. However as all of them had gone to some client I was unable to grant her wish. Mobile phones and pagers were unheard of at that time. When I introduced myself as just an audit clerk, she told me that she has two prospectuses of Company A and B, and wanted to know the best one to invest Rs.50,000/-, a king's ransom at that time. As I had brought shares in both these companies and read both prospectuses well, I immediately suggested Company A, which had a good past record. Today after 20 years the Rs.1000 investment I made in Company A brings me an annual dividend of over Rs.2000 and it can be easily sold in the market for over Rs.180,000/-. Company B was of course bankrupt and the shares have dropped to about half its original value. Unfortunately I do not know who the lady who took advice from me was. It was like Sir Arthur C. Clark not patenting his satellite concept thus losing millions of dollars.

Ups and Downs

I was swift and quick with my foundation stage examinations. The Institute of Chartered Accountants for Sri Lanka held four exams, namely Preliminary, Licentiate, Associate I and Associate II. One had to complete all four to be called a chartered accountant. One who passed the Licentiate was considered an intermediate level accountant. To get this certificate it was necessary to complete a period of articles in an audit firm. After getting through Licentiate one could sign a new two year period of articles to obtain the Associate members certificate once passing Associate II. I failed the Licentiate exam in the first try. But I had completed 3 of the exams of the institute of Chartered Institute of Management Accountants by this time. I suddenly noticed that some of the clerks without any qualifications were getting a salary more than me. I had by now completed my first two years of articles and could not sign the next two years as I had failed in my Licentiate examination. Then one day I approached Mr.Herat and demanded a higher salary. When I inquired as to why those without qualification and who has joined after me were getting a higher salary, Mr.Herat told that I am a trainee and they are not. Of course I am a trainee, getting trained to be a qualified accountant, while the other in question was not. But does this mean that someone who is working and will one day end up as a doctor is worth less than a nurse.

Answering my many queries he told me that I am paid on the basis of someone doing his articles and such a person is someone who is still learning. The person without qualifications is not someone who is learning, but in the final stages of working. He also said that I still have only the first examination of the Institute of Chartered Accountants for Sri Lanka, and that is not sufficient for someone doing his articles to get a high salary. Then I mentioned that I have completed three examinations of the Chartered Institute of Management Accountants, and that is a valuable qualification. Mr.Herat agreed but said that because I am paid on an articles basis that value is not considered. Then my question was as to why I cannot be paid on the basis of my Chartered Institute of Management Accountants basis, for which Mr.Herat said that I could be paid on that basis if I so wish. Not thinking beyond that I told him then to pay me on that basis. In the next month there was a substantial increase in my salary.

Things went on fine until the results of the Chartered Licentiate examination came. I had got through the exam this time. Of course passing an examination is something to be happy about. When you get through your Licentiate examination you can sign for another two-year period of articles after which you become eligible to obtain your full Chartered certificate once all the exams are completed. So I approached Mr.Williams, the partner who is in charge of activities relating to training, and signed the two-year training agreement. When such an agreement is signed the only thing that happens is that a set of forms is sent to the Institute of Chartered Accountants and you become entitled to some stipulated study leave of about one and a half months for an exam. Of course you are not paid a salary during the period of leave. Other than that there is no other perk or benefit. The work that you do will not change, but armed with the Licentiate certificate you are more valuable now.

Life went on as usual. The partying, working, joking and carom playing which were embedded into our lives just continued. I was studying and attending classes for the third exam of the chartered institute. But when I wanted to go on study leave for the examination

Mr.Herat told me that I am not entitled for study leave as I am not a trainee. I told him that I am a trainee and that I have signed articles as I got through my Licentiate examination. Mr.Herat thought for some time and told me he'll speak to me later. Sometime later both Mr.Herat and Mr.Williams called me and said that I have done something wrong by signing a training agreement while getting paid on a Chartered Management accountancy basis. I was totally confused and even you might be confused as to what all this means. I told them that it is a fact that I had got through all those exams giving me the opportunity to enter into pacts considering the levels of examinations that I have got through. But they told me that once someone signs as a trainee he cannot get a high salary, as he is just a trainee and that I had done some sort of cheating. They also calculated and showed me that I have to pay back the excess salary that I have taken during the past year.

I was furious. This I thought was absurd. Then I argued and pointed out that I got the salary because I gave that service to the company. I signed the training agreement because I had another additional qualification and not because I failed some exam. In these circumstances it is not a reduction that the company should mention, but an increase in salary. But they did not budge. They were giants in the accountancy field. Any confrontation would be like war between David and Goliath. But this Goliath did not have a weak spot on his forehead.

Everyone who heard this story fully agreed with me. Their slogan was that this type of unfairness should not be tolerated. Audit firms had the opportunity to get work from people of high calibre for a small fee because of the compulsory training agreements that students had to sign. Everyone wanted me to inform the institute about this and take some action, some even agreeing to bring this matter to the parliament of Sri Lanka. I had support from everyone, and was wondering where I should start my campaign.

During these times my father was abroad. About two days after this incident he came home on a holiday. My father too worked in parliament before he went abroad and I told him the entire story and asked how he will help. His first question was why I joined Williams and Company. The answer was simple; it was to embark on a professional career. Then he asked me why I am worried as to how I reach that point. I had no answer to this question. He pointed out that if someone works as a labourer in a company and suddenly wants to work as a prestigious clerk, he cannot be paid the same high salary he was paid as a labourer, but in the long term the labourer will be benefited because he will reach the peak as a clerk and not as a labourer. Similarly in my case Williams & Company has every right to take back my salary as I am getting a future value from them as an article clerk. My father's argument was that confrontational attitudes are only for the labourers and such attitudes would only jeopardise my future as an accountant. I followed his advice and paid back the excess salary and continued happily ever after. I still value the advice my father gave, as today I have come a long way since that advice.

After some time I also got through the fourth examination of the Chartered Institute of Management Accountants, and now I was armed with CIMA Stage III and Chartered Licentiate. Everyone considered me to be an invincible giant at the speed by which I was going towards the summit. Little did I, and they realise that this is as far as I would go.

It was still the early eighties and suddenly communal tension seemed to be developing in Sri Lanka. In the north the Tamil minority of Sri Lanka were gradually taking arms against the Sri Lankan government. One day in 1983 after an attack by Tamil rebels (known the world over as Tamil Tigers) on a group of army soldiers, communal violence erupted all over the country. All round it was death and destruction. In fact Sri Lanka would have moved back in its forward march at least by 20 years as a result of this incident. It also strengthened the stance of the Tamil Tigers in demanding a separate state for Tamils in the north of the country. The violence also resulted in the Tamils in Colombo losing faith in the majority Singhalese though vandals and thugs carried out these attacks. Most of the employees in Williams & Company also happened to be Tamils. There were many advantages in being in such an environment. The commonly used language in the office was English and anybody joining the firm would very soon improve his English even if he did not know a word of it when he joined. There was also more decency in this type of environment, though I do not wish to give credit to any community that their behaviour is superior to other communities. However after the communal violence the structure in the office also changed gradually and along with it I found conditions deteriorating with more insulting, gossip and brawls.

The communal violence changed the life of many. Though Tamils seemed to be at the receiving end the greatest loser was the majority Singhalese. It took years to start again from scratch. Tourism declined, and the hotel industry completely collapsed. Even today after decades these hotels cannot earn enough money to pay off their loan interest commitment. Many business establishments in Colombo belonged to Tamils and commercial activity came to a temporary standstill leaving us clambering for groceries. Many of the multinational organisations were also gutted down, resulting in even our losing all our audit documents in one such place. Singhalese people also had many businesses to their credit. One of the internationally famous biscuit factories were started by a simple Singhalese villager who came to Colombo to work as a hotel aid. But there were many businesses that solely depended on the monopolistic policies of the previous regime, and after free trade came into practice they fell like skittles in the face of competition.

I saw a clear distinction in the way Tamils do things. For instance in one organisation I saw the director's children working as ordinary clerks in their father's company, under the command of his father's employees. Some day they would of course have to steer the company from the director board, but they have to follow the long way up. This has given them more stability. But some businesses of the Singhalese tended to collapse once it is taken over by its pioneers' children, as the children had no idea of the hardships their parents have undergone to bring the business to this level.

In my experience as an audit clerk I was able to associate many owners of businesses and their top managers and got some understanding on their failures and successes. During my school days we have heard leftist politicians talk about these business men who come to work when they want and go when they want with their whole life being a holiday. The rightist politicians though having solidarity with the businessmen would not utter a word in their favour. Though we clapped with enthusiasm at those slogans now I realise that they would have gone home when they wanted to work till midnight to prepare for tomorrow.

I now had got through Chartered Licentiate and CIMA Stage III. With only one more examination in CIMA I decided to somehow concentrate on that. The exam was conducted every six months and when inquired about my qualifications I would say I am sitting for finals. However after I write for the examination I would tell anyone that I sat for finals. That will be till the results are out. Once the results are out and I know I have failed I will again mention "sitting for finals" as my qualification. This went on for some time until I decided to give up finals and concentrate on my work. To the astonishment of all those who knew me in my heydays my professional career has reached its limit.

I did my work well. In fact putting any company's accounting work in to order was one job I was an expert in. Though we had not yet seen computers, I was entrusted with many such tasks. I always reduced the volume of work mostly created unnecessarily due to lack of planning. I used many examples to justify certain things. One that I keep repeating is the story of the scribe and the labourer. This example is repeated by me to point out that someone struggling with his work is not necessarily doing more work than others. The story goes as follows:

One Merchant was having a labourer to move his merchandise and a scribe to attend to his paper work and accounts. The scribe though relaxed and seemed to be idle most of the time was getting about four times the salary of the labourer. The labourer, unhappy about this always complained to the merchant that this was unfair. The merchant calmly said that one day he will explain the reason for it.

Then one day the merchant saw a team of people in bullock carts moving far away. He called the labourer and asked where those people were coming from. The labourer ran to the people, came running back and told the merchant where they were coming from. The merchant then wanted to know where they were going. The labourer ran back and came and told the merchant where they were going. The merchant then asked why they were going on this journey. The labourer did not hesitate to find out and tell the merchant that they were going to sell their merchandise. The merchant wanted to know what they were selling and again it was a marathon run for the labourer. The demanding merchant wanted to know the price of the merchandise, the quantity and many more things and the labourer was now perspiring and exhausted. The merchant asked the labourer whether he was tired and the labourer said that unlike the scribe who was inside seated, he was able to run up and down and do a lot of work. Then the merchant as if to verify what the labourer said called for the scribe. Once the scribe came the merchant asked the same first question that he asked the labourer, that is where the people far away were coming from, from the scribe. The scribe calmly walked up to the people far away and came back while the labourer looked with a grin to see how the scribe will endure all those trips up to the people far away. The scribe walked up to the merchant and told where the people were coming from, where they were going to, why they were going and many other things which the merchant even did not think of. Then he calmly went inside. The merchant turned to the labourer and asked him whether the scribe did more work than the labourer or not. The labourer did not answer, but now realised that a person tiring himself more does not necessarily mean that he is doing more work.

I always tell my subordinates to know beforehand the purpose of doing something. A good example of doing a job without knowing is found in Sri Lankan folklore where a man named "Kaluwa" went to "Marapana".

Kaluwa was a servant in a posh house in the village. The lady of the house one day wanted to send some foodstuff to her brother in "Marapana". She prepared everything with the intention of sending them to Marapana through Kaluwa. Then deciding to send them the next day she packed them up. However not willing to take a chance, that night the lady approached Kaluwa and told him that the next day he has to go to Marapana early in the morning to her brother's place. Next morning when the lady looked for Kaluwa he was not to be seen anywhere. She thought that in order to avoid going to Marapana, Kaluwa must be hiding. Anyway as Kaluwa has to ultimately come home before dusk the lady waited. In the evening Kaluwa came home. When the lady scolded him for avoiding going to Marapana,

Kaluwa said that as told in the previous day he had gone to Marapana early in the morning and is now coming back.

I have repeated these stories over a thousand times to my subordinates. Some of them have completed all their exams and are now earning 5 times the salary that I get. As I had now decided not to continue with my exams it was not necessary to continue at Williams & Co. There were plenty of employment opportunities for accountants whether fully or partly qualified. While I was thinking of finding employment as an accountant I met Ranil while doing some shopping. Ranil studied at St. Joseph's College. He also joined Williams & Co. and worked as an accounts clerk. He left to join his father to help him in his business. Ranil told me that he was helping his father in his business, but wanted to set up his own consultancy and invited me to join. He pointed out that I am carrying out many assignments which bring about Rs.30,000 to the company while I get something like Rs.3000 out of it. If I take up such assignments and do it on my own the Rs.30,000 will be for me. This was true, an opportunity has come to my feet, why not give it a try? I agreed and Ranil told that he will find some office space.

Ranil found some office space adjoining a large house. It was just one room marbled and polished, and being part of the house, had a prestigious appearance. We bought two tables, opened a bank account and set up shop. I was still employed at Williams and Company and had not thought of giving my resignation as I did not know what the outcome of doing my own business is going to be. We named our company J.R.Consultants, with J.R. standing for Joseph and Ranil, the owners of the company. All ready to get to work we placed an advertisement offering accountancy services with the intention of gathering some clients.

Mind my own business

We had big plans for the future. Ranil as a partner of the company will engage in many other activities like land sales, real estate dealings and sale of motor cars. He will bear the rent of the room and also pay the office helper who runs errands for him. I on the other hand had to pay any accounts clerks that I employed and had to maintain the office with Ranil having no interest in the income from accounting work.

Our first advertisement did not bring any permanent clients. There were few who came for advice on tax matters. But we kept on advertising and we suddenly got a contract form one of the leading firms in Colombo. The contract was temporary to put straight accounts for a period of 6 months. The fee was also reasonable. Using my special talent in raising accounts from any state of chaos, I started working.

I had to give my resignation to Williams and Company. The parting was sad, but ties with the company were not severed. It was like the end of the wonderful life one spends in the university. However someday you have to face the realities in life. Business was not what we thought of during our school days. We had heard at that time, especially from leftist politicians in their meetings, that business people are lucky, as they have no fixed working hours and that they are their own boss and many other stories. However now I realised that every client who comes to you is now your boss. Also I realised that it is a difficult way up with a pot of gold at the end of the rainbow.

The regular and fixed income you normally receive when you are employed was now a thing of the past. You had to work and toil to get income, or starve. The first major client we got was a great breakthrough. However at this point we did not have any staff members to assist me in my work. At this time a friend came to the rescue and provided me with a few university students who will work part time for me. Then I discovered that they are actually looking for some pocket money for a specific purpose and once that is fulfilled will keep away. Suddenly my partner was approached by one of his friends to provide employment for a relative of his and we immediately employed her in our company. This was the first employee of our company though there were others working on a temporary basis. In order to be fair by everyone I have to mention that my cousin, a beautiful girl in her twenties, was the first person to assist me in the initial stages of the company. Later she had to pursue law studies and could not continue working for me. Then a friend of mine brought his brother to Colombo to help me and he later started pursuing an accounting career at Williams and Company and is now a lieutenant in the Sri Lanka army.

Anyway the first real employee of J.R.Consultants was this girl, "Geetha" was here name. Geetha was pretty and had all the qualities of an innocent village girl who has just come to Colombo. This being the first time she had worked anywhere she valued the experience that she would eventually get by working for us. I assigned her to work on the first major accountancy assignment we were working on and she did her job quite well. Having an employee in the company was one step forward.

For those who do not know what accounts are and what these accountants are up to, it is necessary to give a brief explanation as to what we mean by putting a set of accounts in order. As I explained in chapter one accounts provide the means for management to interpret what is happening in the organisation. Just as the bride's father evaluated and compared the individuals A, B and C, organisations will compare between alternatives in order to choose the best course of action for the future. When the activities of the organisation runs into thousands of transactions per day all these transactions are recorded in the double entry system either individually or as a batch and many errors can creep into the system while this is being done. Of course computers were still in the science fiction books for us, though it was a little after the mid-1980s. As a result of these errors, the final list of balances that is extracted from the books namely the 'trial balance' will not balance. In such a case it is not reliable to make any decisions based on accounts prepared from these records.

In correcting such errors it is normally necessary to check all entries one by one to correct the errors. Though it sounds easy when computers were still not in practical use the job was meant for experts and that was the part we were supposed to do. However this was not the service that businesses should get from people like us. Rather than correcting errors of the past our services should be hired to carry out the work without errors. Unfortunately most people hired accountants to correct errors created by other non-professional people. This could be human nature. For instance people go to a doctor when they are sick, but very rarely do they go to a doctor to get advice on how to remain healthy without falling ill.

Gradually we were having a few small clients to keep us going and about four girls were working as accounts clerks. In employing accounts clerks we always gave priority to girls. When carrying out assignments through an employee, the fee is collected by the company, out of which an allowance is paid to the employee. Boys may get tempted to take the entire fee and could negotiate to do the work without involving the company. On the other hand boys had to be under strict control as they had plenty of entertainment around and could leave office to see a movie or for a drink. Girls during these times in Sri Lanka were used to travel from home to office and office to home as a rule.

I had built up a reasonable clientele to keep the business going. I was quite happy with the service I gave for very reasonable fees. The lessons I learnt from the business world were many.

Human nature has various forms. The ability of a person to do his business depends on his nature. As accountants, we advise businessmen on the best course of action which should be followed. For instance if we advise a businessman to build that extra floor to his shop instead of buying a new car, the decision will be made by the businessman. Although we see from calculations and numbers that our decision is more profitable, the mind of the successful businessman has a better understanding of the environment.

There is a chance that buying a car brings in more customers due to the prestige attached to it. This is unfortunately not reflected in our calculations, but yet we learn from experience, in this case the businessman taking the role of our advisor.

Doing your own business was fun. You know that you are rewarded for hard work. I could leave what I learnt about business to a latter chapter. I met many interesting people and the girls who worked for me were so close to me that we were more or less like one family.

A few blocks away from my office there were two other businesses in their infancy. One was a beauty salon for ladies that also distributed cosmetics, run by a lady named June. The other was a real estate agency done by one Siva. Though we had no contact with June, Siva did a lot of business with my partner. His business was still in its infancy and I knew he made a hand to mouth existence. While he was doing business with my partner I too was able to befriend him.

Siva was an interesting person. The word tall would not do his physique proud. He was towering above all. He had a fancy towards the English Language and as he got a kick out using it he kept on talking. For instance this is how he would describe a simple act of waking up in the morning and going to the shop.

"Well, early morning at seven o'clock I heard the sound of birds and I was not sure what birds were making the noise. Without opening my eyes I kept listening to identify the bird. Then I slowly opened my left eyelid and managed to open my right eyelid. My whole body was aching and laziness had numbed my feet. However I barely managed to bend my right foot and push myself towards the edge of the bed. After painstakingly reaching the edge of the bed I slowly extended my left foot out of the bed and bent it in order to bring my sole into contact with the ground ...bla ...bla ...bla", if I write up to his reaching the shop I will not be able to complete my book. Also after finishing this painful and tiring episode he would ask "Did you get what I'm trying to tell you?" to which we have to say yes. Then he will ask "What?" to which my reply is not a decent one.

Siva was a wonderful person. He was simple and honest. He was very keen in building a good reputation and goodwill more than what profit he made. For instance after setting up a foreigner to a house he would skip one meal and use that money to buy a bouquet of flowers for the foreigner as a matter of curtsy. We would always advise him against doing so, but as things are now he has proved us wrong.

He would always travel with me on my motor cycle to cut down on his travelling expenses. His pocket was mostly empty though he could well do a good job as a sales executive in a reputed firm. He was willing to suffer for his future benefit.

Most of the girls who worked for me came from faraway places and I too being a bachelor had to escort them around to help them do their errands in the city. This way they were very much dependent on me and attached to me.

One such girl I will always remember was Madhuri. One day Nalini, a Tamil girl from Williams and company (today she is the director of a company) brought Madhuri with her and asked me to employ her. Madhuri was as beautiful as a Hindi actress from Bollywood, and her figure was a perfect 10. Nalini was a much respected friend of mine and I would never let her down regarding such a request. So I immediately employed her.

Madhuri came from Jaffna and did not have any relations in Colombo. Once she joined my office I found out that though she could do her written work in English she knew only Tamil, a language not much in use in Colombo. I also could not converse with her and had to make some effort to explain things to her in English. On one such occasion I came to office and only Madhuri was in office. I wanted to know which clients the other two girls have visited. Unable to express my question to her I called my friend Siva and asked how I should ask it in Tamil. He told me to ask "Ungalada Enna Virupama?". When I asked her she blushed. The question meant "Do you like me?" However as she was unable to speak Sinhala (the language spoken by Sri Lankans) I had to converse with her in English with whatever effort I could make. She gradually mastered the English Language so well that she joined a prestigious international travel firm where the knowledge of English is very much required.

Even after leaving my office she always came to me for help and called me her sixth brother (or was it seventh) as she came from a very large family.

Sheela was also another girl from a faraway place. She was a tomboy and was fun loving. She really kept everyone happy with her jokes and laughter. There is also a very hilarious incident involving her. One month she took leave for one week to see her mother back at home that was far away. I gave her the leave and she was absent during the first week of that month. During the week I had planned to go to a faraway place with my father by car early in the morning. The trip had to be made on that particular morning and there was no alternative. But the day before I replaced the ball joints of my car and by the time it finished it was very late in the evening. After the new ball joints are fixed you have to take the car to a garage or petrol shed and fill the joints with grease. Petrol sheds are closed late in the evening. While coming back home thinking what to do I saw one petrol shed where they were servicing a vehicle and I turned into that shed to get them to attend to my car too. After the vehicle that was already there finished it was my turn. My vehicle was raised with the hoist and the ball joints were greased giving me great relief to go on the long distance trip. Then I came into the office to make my payment and Sheela was there working in the office. It was amazing how I was destined to come there and meet Sheela who was doing another job while on leave. It is very common for many to go on leave and do a new job so that they can come back if the new job is not satisfactory. No one will know that the employee had tried a new job during her leave. Anyway it would have been a shock for Sheela. Her excuse was that while she was with her mother she got a call to come for a new job and did not have time to inform me. Anyway she gave her resignation, but after sometime joined me again as the new jobs she tried were not satisfactory.

Things were going fine and one day two friends of Ranil who were doing business, approached him to find an office for them to run their business from. As we wanted to cut down costs we suggested that they rent out one of our tables and operate from our office, as what they needed is mainly the telephone and the address.

The person in charge here was Dennis. He was a superb marketer and could sell ice cubes to the Eskimos. He spoke with a phoney English accent, which impressed his customers. We make fun of his accent by imitating one such sentence. "Hello! Mr.Tello, did you come to Colombo to die?" ('Today' sounds like to die in a phoney accent) and the probable answer to the question "Noo, noo, Mr.Dennis I did not come to Colombo to die! I wish to live!"

The only thing Dennis had for his business was the table in our office. He would buy items from producers and supply them to customers playing the role of a middle-man. Yet he had a make believe factory in Timbuktu and a distribution point in Transylvania. He would buy from manufacturers convincing them that they are to be distributed by his own outlet and gives the impression to customers that goods were manufactured in his own factory. He did all the work by himself yet had make believe employees too. The legal officer was Ted Sinclair, the accountant Bryan Muller, the secretary Miss Anne Stephens were some of them. He wrote letters and signed them in different names creating the impression of a large office.

Some manufacturers knew what he was up to, but were not worried as anyway their products were being sold. In fact some of them found that Dennis did better sales for them than their own sales representatives, and they allocated some of their products to Dennis making him the sole distributor for them.

Dennis had an elder brother called Benjamin who would always call him over the phone. When Dennis is not in office he would also tell us to pass the message to him and never forgets to add that the message is very 'urgent'. In fact it had become such a tradition that we nicknamed him 'Urgent Benji'. Dennis was always keen on getting Urgent Benji's messages. Even if he is far away he will come running to answer the phone. We had noted this enthusiasm of Dennis and would always make fun of it by telling him for lies that Urgent Benji is on line. He would not take a chance and would always come to the phone and give us a piece of his mind when he finds out that we have lied. One such day he had walked away from the office and had got into a van of some visitor who had come to pick him up. We got the urge to play our prank and I ran up to the van and told him that Urgent Benji is on the phone. He looked at me furiously, put his hand out of the window and held me by the collar. "Who the hell is on the phone?" He blasted. "Er.. its Urgent Benji." I shivered. "Then who the hell is this chap here with me?" he asked pointing at the person driving the van. "I don't know." I said. But from the way Dennis spoke by now I had realised whom it should be. It was Urgent Benji of course.

Dennis rose fast. One secretary joined his company. After sometime he rented out a separate office and more employees joined. Gradually the square footage of his office increased until he had rented out the entire floor of a building. After some time Ranil too inherited a big business from his father and left to do it full time and here I was all alone with my employees minding my own business.

another book on programming written by a 10 year old kid. On the other hand I used to explain to them about the complexity of driving a motor car. For instance if you turn your steering wheel to the wrong side people will get killed, the vehicle will get damaged and much more. If you do not apply the right pressure to the clutch the plates will get damaged and 10 years of wear and tear will take place in just one hour. Then what about the accelerator and brakes? You definitely cannot take chances with them. But then how is it that every Tom, Dick and Harry can drive a vehicle? High school dropouts and illiterate people too obtain their driving licenses without a problem. Then why should we fear the computer? You can redo what you did wrong. You can erase your errors without a trace. You can re-install what got deleted. These words give my students confidence to start learning. They have always been full of praise for the way I used to teach.

A mistake made by students is that they sometimes mix up what they should know through their earlier education and what they should come to know from the computer. For instance if we ask something like what the final answer to the following command will be the students learn it as if they are learning about computers.

PRINT (7+5)*8/2-6

The result on the screen of the following command will be 42. The only thing in this command that relates to computers is the word PRINT which obviously prints the result on the screen and the * symbol which substitutes the multiplication symbol to prevent it being mixed up with the letter 'x'. How the result of 42 was arrived at is elementary school knowledge, where we learned that the formula within brackets have to be worked out first, then the division, then multiplication, then addition and finally subtraction. So I explain to students this difference, pointing out to them that they are learning computer plus something else. For instance if a student learns how to draw a pie chart on the computer, and also he learns what is a pie chart at the same time, learning about pie charts is not part of computer training.

After some time Dennis who was now doing well in his own office, premises showed a keen interest in buying a computer. So we bought a personal desktop computer for about Rs.60,000/-. It had a memory of 512K (512000 characters). It also did not have a hard disk, and used 5 ¼ inch floppy disks for storage. It had one such disk drive. Along with the computer we got a spreadsheet, word processing and database package. Though this is the first time I had come into contact with such a computer, I was assigned the responsibility of setting it up and training the staff of Dennis's office. It was so simple to me. With a few guidelines I obtained from the supplier of the computer I found the power of the spreadsheet astonishing. Though it was also taught in courses covering a few months, I did not see anything to learn for more than a few days in it.

As far as I could see a spreadsheet was a huge grid containing many rows and columns with the columns marked as A, B, C etc. and the rows marked as 1, 2, 3 etc. Each square was addressed by its column and row coordinates as A1, A2.. B1, B2 etc. It is in this manner that we sometimes name the squares in a chess board. We can enter text, numbers or formulas in these squares. For instance we'll take the following example.

A   B   C

1	Chocolate	50
2	Bread	40
3	Total	=B1+B2

In squares A1, A2 and A3 we have entered text. In squares B1 and B2 we have entered numbers. In square B3 we have entered a formula. To indicate to the computer that what we are entering is a formula we have used the '=' sign. Though what we entered in B3 is =B1+B2, what we get in that square is 90. Now this merely does what the calculator does. But the moment you change B1 or B2 the result in B3 will also change. Is there anything more to learn about spreadsheets? There is. But it is mostly a development of the above bit of information. For instance what you write after the '=' sign in a formula is not computer knowledge but your knowledge of Algebra and Arithmetic.

Word processing was great. But what is so complex in it? For instance in the bad old days people hired experienced and skilled stenographers to do their typing. If you applied less pressure while pressing a key and more pressure while pressing another key, the letters typed will be of different colours making the document untidy. Also when a draft was corrected it had to be retyped and again typing errors could creep into the final letter too. So the person typing had to be skilled. But now what has happened? The computer does all the aligning and decides on the printer impact. Also correcting a draft did not involve retyping and new mistakes could not creep into the document. Therefore I think any idiot could type a document now.

Databases were also easy to understand. The telephone directory is a large database. It is easy to retrieve somebody's telephone number by locating his name which is listed alphabetically. But in the computer it is far quicker. On the other hand we can give the telephone number and locate the subscribers name too.

I came to know many people through my computer classes. Businessmen, professionals, school children and priests were among them. The main advantage for them was they realised that computer programming was not as complex as they thought. Yet I knew that something was missing in my classes. My inability to teach anything beyond BASIC was a shortcoming.

Most of the time those who inquire about computer courses ask whether we teach word processing. It is quite reasonable as there were good employment opportunities for those who could do word processing. Then one fine day a student of mine told me about a computer advertised in the papers and why I won't expand my teaching skills after buying that computer.

The student was correct. It was about time that I ventured into something new. I immediately found the newspaper and called the selling company and asked about the computer. It has a 512K memory. It had no hard disk (hard disks were still a novelty for us in the early 1990's). It was one step ahead of what Dennis bought as it has 2 floppy drives. The capacity of each drive was 720K and they used 3 ½ inch diskettes which was the latest in the computer scene. The cost of the computer was Rs.43,000/-, and I asked whether easy payment terms could be arranged.

The next day a sales representative came to meet me and after an initial payment of Rs.15,000/- brought and installed the computer in my office. Now I had the computer, but unlike the 'ZX Spectrum' which has the BASIC language built into it, this computer needed software. So the next step was to get the software which the selling company promised to give. I asked for the latest spreadsheet, word processing and database packages, which I have not yet even seen. Yet I knew it was going to be easy. So on my way to get the software I placed an advertisement in the papers that I will be teaching those packages too.

After I brought the packages I found that all packages come with built in help as well as special tutorials which is quite sufficient to learn the package without external help. Anyway with the in built help and a few books I was in a position to teach the packages when the students started coming. It was one step forward and now I was teaching in addition to BASIC, spread sheet, word processing and database as well. So I increased the fee to Rs.1000/-.

My accounting work and computer classes were progressing smoothly. My employees were also conducting the classes in my absence. As the fees charged by me was comparatively small some students gave me a valuable gift when they completed the course.

Enter the Virus

The new computer was very handy. It was astonishing how it reduced two days of work to just a few minutes. Days and days of hard work involved with the keeping of records and preparation of accounts was now a thing of the past. Stacks and stacks of paper just vanished and were replaced by a few boxes of floppy disks.

Though I did not have a printer, even looking up at the computer to give some information to clients was quite impressive. With this new addition the students were also benefited. I managed to teach them about spreadsheets, word processing and databases making it as simple as ever.

We had windows. They kept the breeze continuously coming into our office room. But windows, relating to the computer was something we had not yet heard of. Maybe it was available somewhere. Monitors everywhere were monochrome. Some people spoke of colour monitors once in a while. Everything we did was based on DOS, which stood for Disk Operated Systems. Word processing packages could be graded according to the degree to which they are WYSIWYG (What You See Is What You Get). When the article or letter that you have typed is viewed on the screen before it was printed, a WYSIWIG word processor gave a clear picture of what the output is going to be like. But most word processing packages were not completely WYSIWYG. So although computers were used there was much remaining work for the human brain to do.

As my computer knowledge was self-learnt I read many articles on computers and about new developments in that field. One day in the late 1980s I read an article in the Newsweek about computer viruses. It described how two brothers running a pirated computer software shop in Pakistan introduced a computer virus into the software so that when someone tried to copy it the virus will be triggered. The virus is an unfriendly set of commands hidden in a diskette that will automatically make copies of itself from computer to computer when the diskette is inserted. At a defined time this programme will go into action, erasing files and ruining data. However my little computer without a hard disk and without any connection with the outside world was safe from these viruses.

To make use of the free computer time I started accepting word processing assignments on the computer. I had a little bit of a talent as an artist. So my work was very neat. Therefore I did word processing assignments very neatly. Suddenly I found university students coming to me with their project books to get them done on the computer. At this particular time I still did not have a printer. So after what is typed is saved on a diskette, my client has to take me to someone to get the work printed. But the trouble was worth it as my charges were fair and the work was neat. A common feature of the University students was that they all brought their work to me at the last moment, as a result of which work was done under pressure in a great hurry.

One fine day after four days of hard work I took the disks containing the typed files to another office to be printed. The university student was also with me ready to hand over his project to his superiors on the following day. When I retrieved the files instead of the text what I saw was spots and marks and duplicated file names etc. I nearly fainted. The university student started perspiring. All the work of four days was gone. Then I knew that a virus has struck my computer. Anyway the work had to be done. I came back to office and started working late into the night. The work was saved in different diskettes at different stages so that at least one of them might be all right. The next morning without any sleep during the night I managed to get the print outs, retyping what is lost and somehow or other cutting and pasting from different files.

The virus kept me awake for several days. Work was not the same now. We had little knowledge of what to do about it. Then I went to the computer company to ask for a remedy. They checked my diskettes and found them to be infected with a virus called 'Dark Avenger'. They gave me an anti-virus programme to clean my diskettes. After that the virus problem was all right. It was only at that time that I found it important to keep an updated anti-virus programme to counter any future attacks.

Though the virus was no longer there I still had to go to another location to do the printing. Anyway it brought in a good income to the business. The computer classes were also done when the computer was free and accountancy work was also simplified and I could handle more work now.

My office was close to Colombo, the capital of Sri Lanka. I lived with my parents in the suburbs and was not very far away from Colombo. But still I thought it would have been better if I could stay close to the office so that I can come there even at short notice. It was then that one of my friends from Williams & Co. told me that they were sharing an annexe for their studies and invited me to join them. As I was also doing my accountancy examinations I thought of it as a wonderful opportunity and joined them. The place was an upstairs flat with furniture and there were four of us all pursuing a career in accountancy. With two of us having cars and all working in an executive capacity the place stood out among other blocks. We were reserved and among our books most of the time. But the fun and booze was very frequent. We were always visited by our friends, for group studies sometimes during the middle of the night.

It was chaos again! Sri Lanka, in addition to the Tamil Tigers had its own Sinhala Lions. They were followers of the Communist ideology though we are not aware where communism exists. Taking advantage of the inability of the government to suppress the Tigers the Lions too launched their own war. Suddenly the law seemed to break down. There were special announcements made by the Lions to close shops etc., which the shopkeepers always adhered to. Public transport was stopped by the Lions order and I had to transport my employees by car every day. This was going on for some time, and the government struck back violently. The rebels were killed in small groups and their bodies were left on the way side as a warning to future recruits. The police was on the lookout for any suspicious character on the road. It was one of these days that one of our friends was coming to our apartment to do his studies in the late hours of the night. Unfortunately he had to pass the house of a minister of the government that was well guarded by the police.

Our friend was immediately stopped and questioned as to where he was going. Though he knew he was coming to our place he did not know the address of the house. This aroused the suspicion of the police. He was taken to the police and the policemen were very happy to have captured a so called rebel and were already planning for their promotional prospects. Then our timid friend was supposed to lead a huge battalion of cops to our den that was already deemed to be one overflowing with rebels waiting to strike the government the next day.

The cops arrived and my other three roommates were there. But unfortunately, or fortunately I was not there that day to see the fun. My roommates were Cornel, Bastion and Lloyd. It could if necessary be pronounced Colonel, Bastille and Load it. A real battle cry. The cops were geared for war. Cornel was sleeping like the other two. He was closest to the door and the policemen pulled him up from the shoulder. Then the questioning and hunting for evidence started. Coming to know that all of them were top executives may have dimmed their prospects of a raid. Because anyone knows that people will not do revolutions to lose what you have, but to gain something. Then they took into their hands a note book which would give some hint of what is going on. Unfortunately it was written in English and the cop tried to get some favourable clue. The notebook was one belonging to Bastille who was following computer classes after office. The cop could grasp the word night classes and the letters RPG that stood for "Report Programming Generator" a popular programming language at that time. For the policemen the night classes were regarding the future attacks and RPG stood for "Rocket Propelled Grenade". The discovery made the cop very happy. Though he did not run through the streets naked shouting "eureka" he was dancing with glee. Fortunately no one was doing science for if there was a note on the revolutions of the atom, the cops would have thought that the revolution to be launched against the government would ultimately end up with our own atom bomb being hurled at the parliament. The only other thing that they took into custody was our valued collection of Penthouse and Playboy magazines.

When you were taken into custody during these days you always ended up in the wayside, most probably burning among some tires. My friends were also destined to that fate. But for some luck neighbours noticed the incident and as they knew people in high places, they immediately sent messages all round and secured their release the next morning. My friends came back with their notes but the Penthouse and Playboy magazines, were confiscated by the cops. Cornel was full of anger that he decided to join the army and take revenge from the cop who guarded the ministers' house. He joined the army finished his training, but the resulting discipline that he acquired removed all thoughts of vengeance from his mind. His name Cornel well suited his new job that we made up a story that his mother when Cornel was born went to an astrologer to get his horoscope done, and on hearing that one day the child will join the army, named him Cornel, which sounded like Colonel. Although we created the story for fun, we have heard it from other parties as a genuine story as it had spread around so fast.

Freedom cannot be taken for granted. Eligible bachelors had their own problems. They were like sitting ducks, always targeted by parents with daughters. Though I had resisted marriage dodging all onslaughts from my relatives and parents I finally found my immune system failing and agreed to see a prospective bride with my parents. So one fine day when we went to see a girl, I discovered that she was the sister of a classmate of mine with many of her relatives having studied at St. Joseph's College. Soon I was visiting her house regularly and we had a grand wedding to say goodbye to the bliss of bachelorhood.

After marriage I needed more income. So I pooled my resources and bought a printer for the computer that I badly needed for a long time. The demand for my classes was increasing and I had more accountancy assignments coming in. I soon felt that like any business, my business was also reaching a turning point and the initial period of struggle is over. On reaching this turning point I steered it to a completely wrong side. In order to save on rent I moved my office to a room in my wife's house that was close to Colombo.

After moving to my wife's house the office completely lost its professional appeal. I got into the habit of attending to household chores during office hours and rather than my liquidity increasing I found that work was now slower and I was losing much more than what I saved on office rent.

The days of advertising and calling for work were over. My business was now about six years old. There were many lessons I learnt by going into business, which cannot be explained in a sentence or two. Businesses have a life cycle. This is explained by philosophers of management, as something like introduction, growth, maturity and decline. When a business reaches the latter stage of decline new strategies have to be developed to give new life to the business. I was able to give advice to anyone who would like to invest his money in business, as to what course of action he should take.

I provided accountancy work to various types of clients. I saw how new businesses flourished and old businesses crashed. How the attitudes of the owner of the business influences the existence of the business was important. Most of the time businesses changed its path when its ownership changed.

One such business where I offered my services was a long established agency of a reputed manufacturer. The business though dealing in products with a very little margin was sure of a large volume of sales and so had lots of cash flowing into the company. It was over 25 years in business when I was assigned the task of carrying out their accountancy work. At this time the management of the business was mainly in the hands of the children and their father who had pioneered had retired himself from business activities. When I was carrying out my work I noted that the new owner was working very hard to maintain order in the business. Loading goods to a transport van was a painful affair with the owner counting and monitoring all the loadings and even a customer purchasing goods had his bags checked by the owner. Daily banking was equally hazardous with money being counted and rechecked with sales before being taken to the bank. This was not what we have been taught about running a business. So I asked the owner why he is not making use of our accounting skills to monitor his stocks, cash etc. With a proper accounting and control system he can easily get the stock position and compare sales against amounts banked without going through a difficult and time consuming process.

He totally agreed with me. The business was a wholesale one with a very small margin on sales. It was so small that the collection on any day is almost equal to the profit for one year. Because of the reputation the product had with consumers the sales volume was high and the daily collection was a large amount. The owner asked me one simple question. He can hand over the work to a manager and monitor the activities thorough our accounts. But if the manager one day runs away with the daily collection our accounts will show clearly and accurately the sum that has been stolen and missing. But can we help him to recover the lost amount, which is worth one year's hard work. We could not argue with him on that point, as he was very much correct. But I have seen businesses, which delegated the work and trusted others flourish and improve day by day though the risks, associated with delegating is always there.

Ignorance of certain controls can also cause a lot of damage to a business. In accounting it is very important to reconcile accounts. For instance one can keep paying his electricity bills, but to ensure that what is paid is accounted for, it is important to compare what you owe to the electric company, with statements that you receive from the electric company. If not, one can even write out a cheque for the electric company and pay one's own electricity bill from the company's funds. The most important reconciliation of all is most probably the bank reconciliation. It is from this that you find out whether what you deposited is recorded by the bank and whether the value of the cheques that you issue are correctly appearing in the bank statement.

One business of which I undertook to prepare accounts had completely ignored preparing the bank reconciliation. Things had been easy for the manager of the business. He would take Rs.11000 for deposit, but will deposit only Rs.1000. He will simply alter the figure in the deposit slip to convince everyone that the correct amount was deposited. In this manner the manager had made enough money to buy a bus and embark in a profitable transport business.

When we undertook the accounts and began to prepare the bank reconciliation, we could not reconcile the deposit slips with the actual deposits in the bank statements and found that the slips were carefully altered. When the owner of the business was informed of the amount pilfered he took the matter to the police. There was nothing that the police could do. The owner could not prove anything. He can also give someone Rs.1000 to deposit and later alter the deposit slip to Rs.11000 and make a complaint to extort money from an innocent manager. The only thing the owner could do was to come to an agreement with the manager to return the money at least from the profit of the manager's transport business. Sometimes it is so easy to manipulate numbers. For instance altering a cheque written for Rs.8000 to Rs.80000 is child's play.

My business had reached a point where I no longer had to advertise for computer students or accountancy work, because, after over six years in operation, I had built up a strong goodwill. Yet I was in such a situation that I was unable to reap the benefit from the progress that I had made after building a business from scratch.

The Promised Land

My parents were both government servants. They did not believe in business and thought that getting a pay cheque at the end of the month was the best thing that happened to anyone. They said that one in secure in life when employed than when in business. They did not have an answer to the question as to how one can be employed securely in an insecure business. They were just implanted with this thought after working for the government all their life.

Yet they did not dictate to me as regard to what I should be doing. However with a new arrival in the house they got a better majority to advocate their thoughts and were able to convince my wife that employment is much better than business. The negativity created in my wife's mind was able to influence me to reduce my business activities and cut down on my computer classes, and though the business was moving smoothly, I suddenly saw a lack of growth which if it continued at the pace by which it took place in the first few years, I would probably end up as a great business tycoon. But maybe people have limitations as to what they deserve, and I thought that I have reached that limit. It was at this stage that I suddenly received a letter to attend an interview regarding a vacancy in Saudi Arabia for a post which I applied even before I started my business.

Going abroad was something so many were vying for. I had it just coming to my lap at an unexpected time. At that time one of my clients was willing to absorb my employees to his business. So I ambitiously went for the interview. I faced the interview and the written test perfectly and was chosen to fly to the Promised Land.

The day was 31st December 1993. It was another turning point in my life. My childhood dream of becoming a pilot never materialised. But I was coming somewhere close to it. For the first time since I travelled in a domestic flight inside Sri Lanka, I was boarding a jumbo jet plane. My earlier encounter with flight was as a kid and I do not remember anything about it.

On this day things were different. I was grown up and boarding a flight was more or less like a first time experience. The thought itself was thrilling, and it was sufficient to suppress the sorrow of leaving behind a paradise isle along with an infant baby and a wife.

I made it a point to secure a window seat in the non-smoking section, and I noted that the seat was near the wing, which gave me the opportunity to see the wing movements, which were rather interesting. I saw the wing expanding as if to come apart, the engines thundered and we were on our way. I was on top of the world.

I saw the ground getting smaller and smaller, and suddenly we were among the clouds. After some time the feeling of motion vanished and we felt as if we were just seated in a theatre, and so it was until we were getting close to Riyadh, the capital of Saudi Arabia. I was suddenly inundated with disembarkation forms, which I had to fill out for many of the illiterate housemaids who were coming to the Middle East to seek greener pastures. During the flight I remembered that my father was in Saudi Arabia about ten years back and what he had told me. He told me that simply by looking at a woman one could get landed in jail and about hazardous sand storms and unbearable weather. I was too old for him to relate anything about dragons or genies in bottles. Anyway the thrill of travelling abroad drowned any horrible thought, which would have come to my mind.

The landing was smooth, and we were met by one of the company drivers, and left the airport in an overcrowded coach. We were thousands of kilometres away from home. By this time I knew that another accountant, a few salesmen and drivers had arrived from Sri Lanka to start work along with me. We had some very jovial people among us who were able to keep memories of home at bay.

We were all taken to a villa where we were assigned rooms shared by four of us. From then on we tried to relax and feel at home. For lunch we bought something called 'Kapsa' which looked more like coloured and flavoured rice. Though a packet had a good quantity of rice we still had not got used to these new kinds of foods.

Though lunchtime was over we now had to think of our future meals. Some of those who came in our batch knew how to cook. But the majority including me were totally helpless and we were at the mercy of those who could cook. Anyway we had to organize ourselves to prepare food by ourselves. We were in no way willing to eat from outside as it was more expensive and we had come here to save some money.

We all brought our provisions from the shops and got down to cooking. By now everyone in our batch knew each other quite well. We had so many things in common. All of us I presume were a chosen lot and stood out in their respective professions well. We all distanced ourselves from our loved ones and had come here with the sole purpose of earning money. We did not have many luxuries in our homes like washing machines, microwave ovens and even videocassette recorders.

My colleague was soon nick named 'Saddam' for his resemblance to the then leader of Iraq. So I will refer to him as such hereafter. Saddam was a good cook. He was boastful of how the aroma from his stews would arouse even the neighbourhood. Saddam volunteered to do the cooking that night. We were all around him helping him to wash the rice, cut potatoes, vegetables and chicken. He was nearing completion of his task and the aroma from the chicken was tempting as by now thoughts of being secluded from all your loved ones had made one feel desolate and hungry.

Suddenly one of the salesmen came to us and was desperately looking for his washing powder. When we asked him in what he had kept it he said that he kept it in a glass to wash the cups and glasses. Then Saddam panicked. He had mistaken the washing powder for salt and put it into the chicken curry. However we were so hungry that we ignored the washing powder and ate the chicken. It tasted good.

We had a long chat after dinner. We were from all corners of Sri Lanka. Some were sales managers and some just sales representatives. Saddam and I were the only accountants who arrived. Saddam was a more serious character than me. Among the salesmen there was one Wilson who kept us all thrilled with his jokes and antics. That night we slept well. The fatigue and stress of travel made it easy for us to fall asleep.

The next day, the first day of the year we were all taken to our new company. The first of January though so special to us was not an important day in this land. They were more inclined to follow the Islamic calendar and had Friday as a holiday instead of Sunday.

We were welcome by a lot of wonderful and friendly people. They were from so many different countries like Sudan, India, Pakistan, Philippines, Egypt, etc. It was so nice to see people of so many nationalities all at one glance. It was like having the globe in your palm and turning it around.

The first impression of the company was very encouraging. The offices were neat, the people and superiors looked so dynamic and though everything seemed to be working like clockwork, everyone was relaxed and smiling. If there was one thing missing in it was the presence of all those beautiful girls who form a majority in an office back in Sri Lanka.

As a fairly large batch arrived from Sri Lanka there was a comprehensive training and orientation programme arranged for us. The Marketing Manager conducted lectures for us during the first few days. He gave us the guidelines to perform our duties and also to survive in Saudi Arabia. One bit of advice he gave was to keep on working so that we will not be affected by loneliness. He said that being idle would lead to make you think of home and will make life miserable.

As the majority from our batch were salesmen and sales drivers, after some time the lectures were not quite relevant for Saddam or me. So we were segregated and a separate orientation programme was prepared for us. The orientation programme was one where we had to meet key personnel of the company and get an understanding of how that section worked.

The company was a large dairy producer. It could be also categorised as one of the popular dairy companies with a fair share of the market in Saudi Arabia. In addition to dairy milk the company also produced fruit juices and ice cream as well. The production was a neat and advanced process. The packaging though common even in Sri Lanka today, was something new to us at that time.

Another memorable feature of the company was the canteen. The refrigerator was always stacked with the company's products and could be gulped down without limit. Our managers were very particular in finding out whether we were consuming the products until we've had enough.

The Administration of the company was out of this world. It could be attributable to both the system that was in operation and the people who implemented them. The managers were simple and humble, yet knew how to steer the company ahead very well. The administrative system was so effective and fool proof that it did not depend much on the ability of the people. Our job was more or less to stand guard and give momentum to this system, in order to ensure the smooth progress of the company. The accounting procedure was fully computerised, yet the 486 machines, which were in use in Sri Lanka, were not very common. As the profit margins on products were higher than what one could make in Sri Lanka, the company could easily afford a posh environment and modern gadgets.

Whatever the feeling that we had in the days that passed, I thought can be compared to the feelings that Madhuri would have had when she first came and joined my office back in Sri Lanka. Just imagine her coming from Jaffna where only people who were Tamils by origin dwelled and living among the Sinhalese without any idea about the language. However her transition into our society was smooth and satisfactory. Maybe we too will soon adapt to the Saudi way of life.

Some of the things that prevailed here was sort of fascinating. The effort by the government to preserve the Islamic way of life was well supported by rules and regulations and a religious police force dedicated to enforce them. The only religion practised in the country was Islam and even a stamp with a picture depicting a symbol of any other religion was torn away before delivering the letter. In Islam it was sort of mandatory for a devoted Muslim to pray five times a day during a time stipulated by a religious body. Though it was carried out by free will in most countries, in Saudi Arabia there was strict vigilance to see whether the Muslims adhere to these rituals. Therefore keeping a shop open during prayer time was an offence punishable by law. Our basic salary was 1500 Saudi Riyals. This was equal to about 20000 Rupees in Sri Lanka. Rather than buying something for ten units in Sri Lanka, when we bought something for just one unit in Saudi, we got a mental satisfaction that we were not parting away with much of our earnings. But simple mathematics will prove that we were paying about thirteen Sri Lankan Rupees when we paid just one Saudi Riyal for an item.

One day a week the company vehicle takes those who wish to go shopping to 'Batha' an area full of shopping malls and supermarkets. Our first trip to Batha was a memorable one. Back in Sri Lanka, which is following an open economic policy, there was no shortage of what you could buy. However in Batha the lines of shopping malls were overflowing with electronic items. You could choose from many items as if buying vegetables back in Sri Lanka. Most of the people doing their shopping were foreigners and there were only a few Saudis in their traditional garb among them. Ladies were also doing their shopping, dressed from neck to toe in a black gown covering them completely except their faces. The native Saudi women however did not even reveal their faces. Most of them covered even their eyes, except for a few posh Arab ladies who showed off beautiful make up in their eyes.

It was winter in Saudi Arabia. Being used to the tropical climate in Sri Lanka, the cold was unbearable. My fingers were benumbed to an extent that I found it difficult to hold a pen and write. However, we soon got used to the cold. The hot water in plenty and the heaters in rooms helped to some extent. Now we were gradually getting used to the land and were feeling at home. We made it a point to at least play table tennis after work to keep ourselves fit. Gradually our team was getting busy with their duties and got engulfed in their work, but Saddam and I were working together and he did the cooking for me while I did the odd jobs related to cooking. The salesmen were given a common uniform, which was a drawback for them who were used to wearing ties and giving orders to their subordinates back in Sri Lanka. Their duties included driving, washing their sales van and loading and unloading goods from the van. They also had to give on credit to some outlets taking the risk of non-payment all by themselves. Back in Sri Lanka they would use at least five or six people to do a similar job. The thought that came to my mind is why they cannot do this in Sri Lanka and earn all the money taken by about six people, which will be much more than what they earn in Saudi Arabia.

The accounting system of the company was computerised, to the extent of about 90%. The salesmen would load their vans and leave to the market early in the morning. They are equipped with a small computer held in the hand, which resembles a large calculator. All the data relating to the company's products are stored in this computer. When making a sale they raise the invoice using this computer, and for all other transactions with customers this computer is used to raise the relevant documents.

After the day's sales activities they come back to the factory with all the sales data in this computer. Once they unload their goods from the vans they come to the sales office to download the data stored in their computer to the main computer in the office. The sales accountant handles this procedure.

The company has branches all over Saudi Arabia. The branches are distribution centres, which carry out marketing of the products of the main company in their particular area. The same activity that goes on in the head office regarding sales takes place in the branches. There too the salesmen download their data into one computer in the office under the supervision and guidance of the branch accountant.

Once the branch accountants have downloaded all the data they will merge the data and prepare their reports. Then they he will use the telephone line to transfer the data to the head office in Riyadh where the sales accountant prepares his reports for the entire company. Therefore by 12 noon on any day the management can find out how the company functioned up to 12 midnight on the previous day. Much of our training was concentrated around this activity, which was like the heartbeat of the company.

The other functions also were equally streamlined both in terms of the technical and administration aspects. Our orientation program went on smoothly after which myself and Saddam was assigned the task of updating the fixed asset register of the company. In doing so we got the opportunity to move into every nook and corner of the company. As we had to go through records of the company for almost ten years we got a clear understanding of the company's development and its policies throughout the years.

The process of updating the register was organised in several steps. First the books of the company, vouchers and various bills and receipts were checked to prepare a clean list of assets giving its value and description according to the books. Then a through physical verification was to be carried out to check our list with the actual assets available. After that all obsolete and non-existing assets were to be written off and any unrecorded assets were to be recorded in the books.

In doing our work we were directly under the supervision of the Finance Manager and the Accounting Manager. As far as we know they only gave advice and the guidance necessary for us to do our work rather than exercise authority. The Finance Manager was from the Middle East and was dressed in the traditional Saudi dress all the time. The Accounting Manager was a Sudanese, humble and quiet, speaking only when it was necessary in a very poetic form. Like the rest of our superiors they too made sure that we were happy and got what we wanted.

Journey to Al Baten

We were still in the first month of our arrival in the Kingdom. The salesmen were now going around Riyadh in their sales vans to distribute the products of the company. We all cooked together and enjoyed a chitchat after dinner. The country was free of booze and the only thing we had was non-alcoholic beer, which was okay as long as you drank only one bottle. The second bottle would remind you that it is non-alcoholic and so we normally stopped at one bottle.

Sri Lankans (and maybe many Asians) are famous for their hot spices, which they mix in abundance with their food. Some westerners say that Asians were not in the habit of using toilet paper, as there was a risk of it catching fire when being used. The main and hottest such ingredient is chillies. Before mixing with your food the chillies are dried, grounded and the powder is fried in a pan. This gives a very hot aroma, which only a devil or an Asian can tolerate. In one such instance one of the Sudanese salesmen who were staying in the same villa with us ran from the scene nearly choking to his death.

All of us were not supposed to remain in Riyadh forever. We all knew that we were to be sent all over the Kingdom of Saudi Arabia after getting familiar with the country. Then after about a one and a half months, Wilson and Bertie, two Sri Lankan salesmen were told to take up duties in Hafer Al Batin, a city about 500 kilo meters away from Riyadh and very close to the Kuwait border. We had a small farewell party. Though we knew each other for just one month the parting was sorrowful, mainly because Wilson entertained us all.

After arriving in Hafer Al Batin both Wilson and Bertie wrote a long letter to us describing their horrible experiences before settling down in Hafer Al Batin. First of all they had been waiting at the Riyadh airport when an official called out to people who are waiting to board the Hafer Al Batin flight. Then Wilson and Bertie had happily boarded the plane. Unfortunately Hafer Al Batin airport is the one reserved for passengers going to the King Khalid Military City. The airport used by passengers to Hafer Al Batin is the Quisumah airport. But how can one know without extra sensory perception. After disembarking at the Hafer Al Batin airport our friends were happily waiting for someone to come and pick them up to be taken to their accommodation in the depot. However they soon witnessed that everyone was moving very swiftly and a lot of military personnel were present. This was so different from the relaxed atmosphere that they witnessed back in Riyadh. Everyone around spoke only Arabic, and they were unable to find out where they were. There was no one expecting their arrival. Suddenly one official they understood were probably asking them to leave the place as soon as possible. Then they got into a taxi and told the name of our company which the driver understood and Wilson and Bertie were taken to Hafer Al Batin and handed over to the former agents shop in the heart of the city. Their misery had not ended yet. Other than some Indian shopkeepers there was no one at the agents shop at that time. But at least the Indians spoke English and they told them that the owner of the shop will arrive soon.

When the owner of the shop (the former agent of the company for that area), a Saudi national arrived Wilson and Bertie were devastated with hunger and they put it all out blaming the agent for not meeting them at the airport and for the delay in meeting them. The agent understood their anger and their hunger and first took them to his restaurant and made sure that they ate well. To their amazement our salesmen also found out that the agent spoke very good English and was one of the business tycoons in the area. When the company's own manager a Sudanese national met the salesman they were well fed and calm. However episode two of their horror story was about to begin.

The salesmen were taken to their accommodation and they saw hell on earth. Though some nationals tolerate anything as long as there was a roof over their head, it was not as such for Sri Lankans where even the poorest of the poor build good houses with marbled floors and modern facilities. Even foreigners who come to Sri Lanka look for dream houses with landscaping and indoor gardens to enjoy the difference from the tenements and line homes in which they live even in well developed countries. The apartment reserved for the salesmen was a house, which was formerly a video centre, and the place was overflowing with old videocassettes. The toilets were also overflowing and the stench was horrible. Once again the salesmen were furious. The salesmen demanded that they be sent back to Riyadh or to Sri Lanka immediately. This gave a rough idea to both the manager and the agent as to what standards the Sri Lankans expected and took immediate action to clean up the place and hand it over in good condition. After that the place was cleaned up and carpeted and then the salesmen were able to settle down.

Then the salesmen wrote to us about the depot manager who was not officially given the designation of manager yet. They found him to be humble and simple exercising no authority at all. Work in the area was wonderful as it was a new depot and the work was challenging. The salesmen had the freedom to make decisions and to play an active role in the management of the new depot. This was no difficult task as they were smart workers even back in Sri Lanka where the market is very competitive and challenging. The regional manager, who though exercising some authority mostly educated the salesmen about the way things has to be done in Saudi Arabia, visited them from time to time. Another thing that they wrote about was that they both were suffering from hernia after loading and unloading their Lorries all by themselves. Anyway overall they didn't have anything else to say.

We got used to the parting of our friends and the cold climate gradually. Now we were doing our work and Saddam and I were occupied with our work related to fixed assets. We used to switch on heaters and wear heavy clothing to avoid the cold. We got so used to the dress that we did not feel the cold climate gradually departing and the rising of the temperature. Only when everyone was inquiring as to why we wrapped ourselves in so much clothing that we realised it was getting hot.

Hafer Al Batin was functioning without an accountant. The manager of the depot was a good salesman and knew how to increase sales and had a smile, which will make any shop owner buy our stuff. But accounting was a little more complex than that. So the sales management was requesting the finance management to send an accountant to the depot as soon as possible. Another Sri Lankan accountant who was in the company for some time was supposed to go to Hafer Al Batin. The accountant at that time was stationed in Abha, a town in the hills where the climate was always cool. As he was experienced and the depot in Hafer Al Batin was a new one it was the most appropriate thing that the accounts department could do. However there was a delay in doing so as the work in Abha was not yet assigned to a new accountant. This piled up the work in Hafer Al Baten and the sales management insisted on sending accountants immediately to Hafer Al Baten and another depot in Hail (pronounced 'high ill'). I and Saddam were the only spare ones available in Riyadh. We were immediately told to get ready to depart, myself to Al Batin and Saddam to Hail. Hafer Al Baten was 500kilo meters away from Riyadh. A flight takes about 45 minutes to reach the Quisumah airport from which one has to reach the Hafer Al Baten town. Unfortunately air tickets were all booked and it was not possible to get one at the last moment. The next alternative was to go by bus. Since buses were also scheduled to depart a little late the best way to travel was to go by taxi. So a company official escorted me to the taxi stand and introduced me to a taxi driver and his assistant who spoke only Arabic. I and a Bangladeshi who were travelling to Hafer Al Baten shared the rear seat. The Bangladeshi spoke Arabic and a very little bit of English. This was enough for me to strike a small conversation and learn a few Arabic words.

I was about to begin the longest journey I had so far travelled in a motorcar. The taxi driver was a pleasant old man and his assistant was a young boy. You needed an assistant maybe because of the distance we were travelling. They could take turns driving the vehicle and nobody will get exhausted. The car was a 16 cylinder Chevrolet and had a smooth noise like the buzzing of a bee. It was large and was comfortable and you felt so light in the seats, almost as if you were travelling by aeroplane. The road stretched far ahead and you could see the horizon. I wondered how long it would take to reach Hafer Al Baten. I had driven even my motorcycle at 100 kilometres per hour back in Sri Lanka. However that was the fastest speed I could imagine on the road. Neither my bike nor my car could accelerate beyond that even if I wanted to. But now I was travelling 500 kilometres and an old man was driving. I could see large containers and tippers overtaking us by the dozens. I estimated the speed of the vehicle to be about 40 kilo meters per hour, and looked forward to nearly half a day cramped inside a car. As we were moving at this speed I just thought of raising my head above the driver's seat to see the speedometer. When I saw the speedometer I could not believe my eyes. We were moving at a minimum of 150 kilo meters per hour. Because of the size of the car and the emptiness in the surrounding area it was not possible to feel the speed of the vehicle. The other large vehicles would have been travelling much faster. In addition to the distance I was experiencing a speed, which I had not experienced on the road before.

The government of Saudi Arabia was very much concerned about the security of the country. So many vices, which were common headline news back home was almost non-existent here. The government was also dedicated to preserve the Islamic way of life from outside influences. So, security checkpoints were maintained and one was not allowed to go from town to town without the proper papers. When we came to half way between Riyadh and Hafer Al Baten, we too were stopped to check our papers. It was here that I found out that I did not have proper papers to go past the checkpoint. The policemen were explaining to the driver that I should turn back to Riyadh. It was out of the question with the taxi going towards Hafer Al Baten. However with the little Arabic I learned from the Bangladeshi in the car I told that it is what a Saudi company has given to me and therefore it was not my fault. After much convincing the policemen allowed me to go past the checkpoint. I had made my entry into the atmosphere of Hafer Al Baten.

The whole journey took about five and a half hours. I did not feel tired. As it was night I went to one of the best hotels in the area. I was given instructions by the management not to move into the company accommodation until I was sure I would be comfortable. However thousands of kilometres away from home I was longing to join my colleagues even in hell. I ate well and slept well and late in the morning I heard a knock on the door. I opened the door and the manager of the depot was there in a simple dress, which Muslims normally wear to go for prayers giving a simple and genuine smile, a smile that totally agreed with his name, Ismail. I was so happy to know that I am no longer alone. I got into his single cab vehicle and came to the company's storeroom. There I saw Wilson the joker of the crowd loading his van. I just laughed in seeing him as even when loading the van he looked like a clown. He was overwhelmed with happiness in seeing me. He knew that life was going to be very pleasant in the course of work. Later we came to our accommodation, which doubled up as an office. In fact my office table was in my bedroom. Bertie too was happy to see me and we decided to cook together as we did during the initial days in Riyadh.

The next day we went to our store where all the products were kept. The salesmen did their loading once in the morning and once in the evening. The working hours were from 8 to 12 in the morning and 4 to 8 in the evening. Though a 4 hour gap was there in between, this resulted in a somewhat 12 hour working day. It did not matter very much as life was moving very slowly in the kingdom and the work was not strenuous or stressful. After work we drove around town in the sales vehicles to see the area and to plan our future purchases from the well-lit shopping malls which displayed a wide range of electronic items.

Wilson had very superior people skills. He would make friends all over town. Though his friendships do not last long we had friends all over town as a result of their initial friendship with Wilson. Bertie was reserved and cautious. He had been a friend of Wilson even in Sri Lanka and knew his strengths and weaknesses well. Anyway the three of us made a wonderful team and teamwork resulted in the sales of our company increasing two fold in a short period of time.

We did not have telephones in the stores or villa. As the depot was a new one everything was done manually and a computer was not there even for me to type a letter home. This was a bit difficult for me to endure as I had got used to the computer so much back home. Anyway I managed to do my best with the available resources, to the satisfaction of the management. As we did not have a telephone I had to call the head office from a telephone booth and report on what is going on. We had a toll free number and we did not have to use coins at the telephone booths. However long conversations were not possible as a long queue of people wait at the telephone booths for their turn. Always at the telephone booths coin sellers will provide the necessary change in coins charging a commission of ten per cent (they will give nine riyals in coins in exchange for a ten riyal note).

Close to our villa a Sri Lankan named Rajiv was running a vehicle repair centre in partnership with another Saudi national. Foreigners who wished to do business had to form a partnership with a Saudi national by law. He was a regular visitor to our villa and has been in Saudi Arabia for nearly ten years. From him we got some tips on survival in the kingdom. We noticed that whenever we see a Sri Lankan we could remember seeing him somewhere before. But Rajiv explained that as the foreign faces were different a face of a Sri Lankan stands out among them giving us an illusion of seeing them before. Another valuable point that Rajiv told us was that everyone comes to the kingdom on a short term plan but they get stuck in the desert for the lack of financial planning and inability to achieve their targets. So they keep postponing their stay until the next year which will always remain next.

Rajiv told us that he spends nearly 2800 riyals for a month to call home as he has international direct dialling facilities. 2800 riyals was a lot of money. Enough to buy a good second hand car back in Sri Lanka. I then asked him what the cost of a return air ticket to Sri

Lanka was. I too knew that it was only 2300 riyals. As he was the owner of his business there was no one to command him and he was free, to work as he wanted. So I asked him why he won't visit Sri Lanka once a month and see his loved ones in person without wasting money on telephone calls. He realised his folly at once and stopped calling home liberally. He also did not visit Sri Lanka and saved more money enabling him to anticipate an early return to Sri Lanka for good.

Another good friend we had was Sam. Both Rajiv and Sam had their own vehicles and would visit us whenever they can. Sam was doing a prestigious job in the Saudi Electric Company, which was considered as a good paymaster. However he was still stuck in the Kingdom for nearly ten years as he was building a palatial house back in Sri Lanka.

Our friendships were not restricted to Sri Lankans. We befriended people of all nationalities and learned basic words from their languages. Our friends included Indians, Filipinos, Bangladeshis, Nepalese and Pakistanis. Most of them were introduced to us by Wilson. Unfortunately none of them were female.

Sandstorm

Life was now normal for us as we had got used to the Saudi way of life. We enjoyed the food, which was not hot like back in Sri Lanka. Riyadh was more or less like a part of India. If you walk in the corridors of the shopping malls you can see about ten or twenty Saudi Nationals, dwarfed by the masses of Indians. In Hafer Al Batin things were different. You could see Saudi nationals all round you. The women were covered from head to toe, with even their eyes covered by a veil. Some ladies showed off their eyes with posh make up, glittering like jewels seen through a small window. At least 99 per cent of the people did not speak any language other than Arabic. So gradually I learned to get about using Arabic to converse with others.

My duties were multiple in nature. In addition to maintaining accounts, being the only person other than the manager to administer the depot, I had to perform the duties of a storekeeper, cashier etc. Since the depot manager was inexperienced in administration I also had to guide the salesmen and help them in whatever way I could. As the depot was newly started we did not have computers yet. This was a major handicap for me as I was always with the computer back home. This did not prevent me from writing letters to my friends and family back home. As we were all alone in a desert land, with no entertainment whatsoever, the letters that we wrote went into great detail and were lengthy. In our letters we always emphasised on what we found fascinating in Saudi Arabia. Something that is not heard of in Sri Lanka are sandstorms. So I would always write home about how we walk through sandstorms. But later I discovered that what I had seen were just some sand being swept away for the wind. One day I was thrilled to see and know what a real sandstorm was.

It was midday and we were in the store when the manager said that a sandstorm was coming. I looked outside to see the usual blowing of sand from one place to the other. But that was not what I witnessed. I saw far away a huge wall of sand completely covering the area from the ground to the sky. From this side of the wall onwards it was clear as usual. We saw that the wall of sand was slowly moving towards us engulfing everything in its path. This was my first encounter with a sandstorm. I was thrilled to see what a real sandstorm looked like. When it was coming towards the store we closed all the doors and stayed in the office room. Still we felt the extra heat generated by the storm. The sand crept into the store and office through whatever opening it could find. After about an hour the temperature came down and the sandstorm was gone. It left a thin layer of sand on everything. The sand was more like a powder and did not take the form of small granules or crystals as it is back in Sri Lanka. Therefore it could be easily removed with a vacuum cleaner.

One day we got caught to a sandstorm while I was taking a ride in a sales van. Since we thought it was safe in the van we just parked it by the pavement with the windows closed. This was a good opportunity to get a better view of the sandstorm, so we waited. Once the sandstorm came we found that inside the van where we were seated, dust was flying everywhere. We tolerated it blaming the improper window seals in the van. After about twenty minutes of suffering, I got sick of the situation and asked Wilson who was beside me why these windows can't keep the sand out. While asking this question I touched the glass window next to me. But instead of my hand resting on the glass it went right outside into the open. Then I realised that the window was fully open and as such we thought it was fully closed.

Every day I had to go to the bank to deposit the cash collected from the previous day's sales. I took this opportunity to see around the town, have lunch and to do any other personal work like remitting some money home. Even though I did not know Arabic I did not feel uneasy, but felt quite at home. I found the Arabs to be very simple and pleasant people. It was quite fascinating of them to greet everyone whom they met by saying "Salaam Aley Kum". To this we have to return the greeting saying "Aley Kum Salaam". Then the first person will ask "Kai Fa Haalak" which means something like "How are you?" to which the reply will be "Al Hamdulla, Kwais", which means I am fine with gods belessings. Beyond this the first person says something like "Siloneck" as I can remember. The reply to this is something like "Tyfe". Sometimes the ordeal ends there. But if you don't move on it might go on to "Kaif intha abu" which means "How is your father?" and will continue as a never ending chain.

Bertie was young, but took a serious attitude towards life. Wilson was playful and lived the moment. Both of them were wonderful salesmen. Wilson had a serious weakness that showed. In our case the weakness did not show. Wilson tried his best to befriend the Sri Lankan women who worked as housemaids in almost every other house in the area. Another of his targets were the hospitals where Sri Lankan girls worked as nurses and janitors. Meeting a member of the opposite sex was taboo in Saudi Arabia. Only relations and a married couple had the right to talk to each other. However many Sri Lankans overcame this taboo by posing as a relative of the house maid. Wilson started on his venture by writing his address in small chits and throwing it at house maids while driving his sales van. He had a good response from the ladies. But his most enchanting letter came from someone working with him. It was me.

Knowing about his ambition to befriend a girl I thought of writing him a very provocative letter. The following letter was what I composed.

Dear Bro,

I was so much enchanted to see you drive through our alleys in your majestic van every day. From your looks I knew definitely that you are a Sri Lankan just like me. So many boys were after me when I won the village beauty contest three years ago in Sri Lanka. But I was always looking forward to having a friendship only with someone who was financially stable, even if it does not necessarily end up in marriage. I always come out of the house when I hear the horn of your van. However that day when you threw the paper at me I thought you were teasing me. But when I saw your address written in the paper I became the happiest girl on earth. I immediately ran to our madam and told about it. She was very critical and asked why I did not call you and invite you home. She told how helpful it would be to have a Sri Lankan friend to help me when I want to send some money or gift home.

My madam speaks English and her elder brother is in America. They do not approve much of the Saudi laws and are liberal and westernised. Her husband was old and died last year when she was only 35. We also have a Philippine housemaid who is younger than me to look after our madam's 3 year old baby. Our madam's brother visits us at least once in 3 months. So only the three of us and the baby are at home. So if you can visit me I can prepare some nice Sri Lankan dinner for you once in a way.

So my dear bro, as I am longing to see you and my patience is reaching its limit please meet me tomorrow at the same place where you gave me your address.

Your sweet baby from Sri Lanka,

Nirosha Pushpamali

The letter was written with slanted handwriting, which was different from mine, sealed in an envelope and posted to the address where we all lived. The letter arrived in two days and I saw Wilson reading it with much enthusiasm. Suddenly he jumped up cheering and embraced all of us. He was boasting about his new accomplishment, but he hid the details in the letter from all of us. He told us how first thing next morning he was going to meet the damsel of everybody's dream. But little did he realise that after distributing his address to nearly hundreds of girls spread over about 5 square miles, he will never be able to find out which girl wrote the letter. So for the rest of his stay in Saudi he desperately looked for Nirosha, the girl that was created by the Frankenstein devil in me.

Wilson and Bertie were in charge of two different areas in Hafer al Batin. Both areas had equal sales in the past and so they both got equal targets to achieve. Bertie was a serious character and worked hard to achieve his target. Wilson took things cool, was much relaxed but always achieved his target. This was a strange phenomenon and we all discussed among ourselves how this could be. Everybody's opinion was that Wilson has got an area with a higher sale potential and it was easy to achieve the target in that area. Even I did not know the reason at that time but after observing the situation for some time I knew what was happening.

The way everybody looked at the above situation was a mistake I notice taking place even today. Another such example was taking shape back in Riyadh. When a salesman went on a month's vacation a substitute was carrying out the sales in that area. During that month the sales in the area doubled. After the salesman came back sales figures went back to the earlier level. How did the substitute salesman do double the normal sales volume? The explanation given by most was logical. As it was only one month he has virtually dumped goods into the outlets thus doubling sales. But when the salesman came back he could not do the same because the outlets were overstocked already. Then why can't this salesman choose one month at a later time and double the sales and show that even he could do it. But he cannot. Because he does not have the skill or ability to do it. When we observe something good happening we are reluctant to come to the conclusion that it is happening that way because an exceptionally good person is handling it. But the person in charge of the situation is the main reason why things happen well or don't happen well.

It was also the reason behind Wilson achieving his targets with little effort. He was a salesman par excellence. He had people skills. He had friends all over town. He knew the art of getting round the purchasing manager in the big time buyers. For instance while Bertie ran high and low and exhausted himself doing his sales, Wilson will befriend a purchasing manager and invite him to our villa and throw a party in his honour. Once he becomes very friendly with the manager he will convince to him the value of buying a container load of goods rather than buying them piece by piece. With this one fourth of his monthly sale is done in just one day.

Whatever it is Wilson was a hot favourite among the housemaid community. Sometimes there were conflicts between them to share him. At least ninety per cent of the housemaids had a lover who posed as a brother or relative in Sri Lanka to gain permission from the Saudi master to keep company. Some who had many lovers had to find alternative methods to meet. But they were happily married back in Sri Lanka. However having a boyfriend from Sri Lanka was not a wise thing for a housemaid to do. Most of the time the boys drained the money from these poor girls and left them penniless when the maids had to come back to Sri Lanka. Most probably, back in Sri Lanka they told horror stories to their husbands of masters who did not pay them a salary. The more far-sighted maids always choose an Indian, Pakistani or Bangladeshi for a boyfriend. People of these nationalities shower the maids with gifts and sometimes suggest marriage although the maid has a husband and many children back in Sri Lanka. There is also the advantage of no one coming to know about the affairs and she can always come back to Sri Lanka as a very chaste woman.

Once in a way some unlucky damsel will end up in jail as a result of a love affair. In Saudi Arabia it is prohibited for unmarried couples to freely associate each other. It is an offence, which if committed you could end up in jail. The religious police is very careful in prosecuting such cases. They would follow the couple for some time and will most probably catch them when they are naked in a room. However once in Sri Lanka we will hear a story that they were ruthlessly bundled into a police van while chatting in a supermarket.

Our sales volume was growing fast. And a new stores, office and residence was being put up in another location. We moved into it once it was complete. It was also equipped with our own telephone line. Our friends who were close to our earlier workplace did not stop visiting us although we were a bit far away from them now.

After we moved to the new place the sense of working in an office was there as the office was separate and attached to the store. Another new experience that we encountered was the telephone line. I being the only person in the office most of the time was inundated with telephone calls from Sri Lankan housemaids. This was as a result of our number being distributed by Wilson and also through gossip giving details of us and our office to everybody. Though it is not the case most of the time I always was decent with them and was careful in what I was saying. Conversations were sometimes provocative suggesting times when it was possible to meet and complaints of loneliness. One Sri Lankan in Riyadh was befriended by a girl over the phone and girl was always pestering him to send a photograph. He told the girl that he has one in which he is wearing just a sarong (a cloth wrapped round the body). The girl still wanted it saying that what he was wearing is not important. He then told that he was wearing a sarong and was also standing on his head. Afterwards the girl did not pester him for a photograph.

Although the company was using a wonderful computer system to monitor its progress Hafer Al Batin was using a manual system up to now. As we needed the telephone line to send the data to head office the management did not bother to send computers until a telephone line was available. Finally with the telephone line being fixed the computers were also sent for our use. Things were very easy now. Work was just a matter of fixing wires from the salesmen's computers to download their daily sales data, merging them and sending them to the Head Office next morning through the telephone line. However the telephone ran a long distance along the ground to a house a little far away and we had to fix it most of the time as it broke when it got entangled onto something that went over it.

Altogether the depot had a five man team working for it. They were myself, the manager Ismail, Bertie, Wilson and Fareed who arrived after everyone else as a stores helper. Except the manager the rest of us were Sri Lankans. So we made sure that we had a wonderful time.

Once in a while we would invite all the Sri Lankans around and throw a party. Though singing aloud and even playing loud music is not tolerated in the Kingdom. But in some neighbourhoods the Saudis around ignore it. Also within our small domain we had our own way. The Lankans who gathered had diverse talents. Those who were experts in cooking were the most wanted for a party. We also got the opportunity to mix with people of all walks in life back in Sri Lanka. Though some were fortunate, everyone was not. For some the accommodations were like pigeon holes, and some were not getting a regular salary either. Anyway everyone tried to make the most of their stay in Saudi Arabia as they had to take home something to compensate for the misery that they are undergoing.

Fareed was a bit of a rebel. When in Riyadh he had made a big issue of being unable to stay on the second floor of a villa during fasting time, as the aroma of the food prepared downstairs is tempting. This made the management shift everyone from villa to villa so that Muslims will occupy one villa. Anyone making an issue on religious grounds always had the upper hand in the Kingdom. This action by the management had created the impression in Fareed that he was now above the management. So one fine day when he was told to visit some shops in the area by the depot manager, he wrote a letter to Riyadh stating that he would resign from work. Not having a knowledge of how a company is administered, little did he know, that his letter will not be rejected by management. So when he got the reply accepting his resignation, he was devastated.

Fareed lost his head and acted weird afterwards. He tried to get into a quarrel whenever he could. However with no one been provoked by his actions one fine day when Wilson was spending the weekend with another Sri Lankan friend, he informed the police that they were consuming liquor in that address. The police broke into the address where Wilson was staying and having found no liquor took Wilson and his friend into custody for questioning and cross examining. By this time another salesmen had joined our team as Ice Cream Salesman. Unlike the majority of us he was an Indian Muslim named Maharoof. He was also the salesman I referred to earlier in this chapter, who doubled the sales of an area when he went as a relief salesman for one month. Though he was jovial and had a good sense of humour, the previous day he had an argument with Wilson over his playing his cassette player a little loud. So our immediate response after Wilson was freed from police custody was to suspect our Indian friend. He did not notice until after a long time that everyone else including the manager were avoiding him and talking among ourselves keeping him at a distance. Later he noticed and having come to know the facts swore that he would never stoop to the level of doing such a thing. After sometime we found out from the police that it was Fareed who was behind this. Anyway since we knew Fareed will soon be leaving us we did not make a big issue of it.

Tomato Marbles

I was very much occupied with the computer. It had a colour monitor unlike the monochrome one I had back home. The first thing I did was to install as many games as possible to relax during work. The computer did not have windows installed, but used the old DOS system. Yet it was a step ahead in my computer life.

My other pastime was to tease Wilson. He provided us with enough actions to make fun of. One thing I remember was the day he brought tomatoes. I saw him take a bagful of them to the refrigerator. But the next day when he was bringing it from the refrigerator we heard a Ding Dong sound in the bag. Thinking that the bag was full of crystal balls we emptied it to see that it was the tomatoes. Wilson had put them in the deep freezer and they had hardened into round balls of ice.

Another incident that we remember is one involving the vacuum cleaner. I sometimes fix the vacuum tube in the reverse so that I can blow some dust from the top shelves. Once I did this but forgot to fix it back in the normal suction mode. Wilson took this vacuum cleaner and started vacuuming the floor while it was fixed in this reverse blow mode. When I pointed out what he was doing he did not admit but showed me how the vacuum still removes the dust. Of course he was correct. When the mouth of the vacuum was kept on the floor it blew the surrounding dust far away creating the impression that it was sucked in. Then I took the tube up and kept a paper to the mouth to show to him that the vacuum was actually blowing and not sucking the dust in. This time he saw the light and got me to fix the vacuum in the proper way. This became the talk of the day for some time. Wilson would lose his temper and shout at the top of his voice which rather than creating fear in us, simply added to the fun.

Time was going very slowly and I was entitled to a vacation after one year. Half of the first year was over and we had come to the month of October. Suddenly I saw raindrops fall and later we had torrential rains in the desert land. The roads had no system for drainage of water and the water had to be pumped and removed by vehicles with built in water tanks. We enjoyed the rain as it reminded us of back home where the month of October brings heavy rain. After a few days of rain towards the end of October early morning a visitor came to the office. He was covered in Jerkins and wool clothing like an Eskimo. When I asked him whom he wants to meet he gave a big smile faintly visible through the scarf covering his face. It was our manager Ismail. When I asked him why he was all covered he asked whether I don't feel the cold. It was then that I realised that the climate was unbearably cold. The climate has changed in just one day.

We had identified the Sri Lankan in Saudi into two categories. They were the Eskimos and the Red Indians. The Eskimos hated the hot weather and loved the cold season. They were mostly those working in the open air where the scorching heat during the middle of the year is unbearable. But people like myself loved the hot season compared to the cold weather. Therefore it was a time of suffering for me. I wore the thickest of clothes and switched on the heater in the office. But life went on and we had our bit of fun in spite of the weather.

The depot operated without a helper in the store. This was a big problem for me. When customers came directly to the store there was no one to load the goods for them. However I had befriended most of the customers and there was no way I could disappoint them. So I helped to load the goods for them. As a lost sale meant lesser commission for the salesman I just could not let the customers go. Therefore I even mastered the use of the fork lift truck to help load the customers vans. The company had strict rules that non-salesmen should not handle the products, but I could not help it.

Wilson and Bertie were lucky to have me around. Wilson, though a playboy was very careful with his finance and planning. I was there to give them guidance as to how to save etc. Other than the trouble of facing some locals who came to us to complain about Wilson giving his address to their maids, Wilson was methodical in his work and this made things easy for me. Bertie was also careful about expenditure and was saving his hard earned money. But he spent a little bit for smoking which would have made him a little stingy when spending on food. He also had his elder brother's wedding coming up which would have eaten into his savings a little bit. The preparations for the wedding were going on in Sri Lanka and Wilson was keen on attending it and requested leave. Though the management did not refuse they did so in the last moment and this made Wilson give his resignation. Though I knew his intention to resign I had no reason to talk him out of it. He had collected enough money even to start a small business back home. The only other thing he needed was the determination and the dedication. Later he wrote to us saying that he made the right decision at the right time. He had given out some shops on rent and had started a small distribution. If he stagnated in the Kingdom for too long he would have lost his contacts and skills by the time he went to Sri Lanka.

The time for my annual vacation has already passed but I could not go home as it was not possible to find a replacement for me at that time. However some new recruitments were made and suddenly I was told from head office that my vacation will be in one months' time. An important thing to be done when your vacation is due is to prepare a big box of goodies to be taken back home. Though the essentials were available in Sri Lanka, it was a bit of a fad to bring all the electrical goods from Saudi Arabia as you get a duty free allowance for what you bring. This gives a small cost benefit to the person bringing the goods rather than buying it from Sri Lanka. However now I realise that it is much more economical to bring money and buy the things from Sri Lanka as the difference is nothing much. The other benefit in buying from Sri Lanka is that the goods imported are sometimes custom made to suit the climate of the country. Then there is the advantage of the guarantee card and also there is no risk of the goods being damaged while in transit.

Everyone from around gives things to be taken to their loved ones back home. There was a lot of solidarity among the Sri Lankans that it was a moral duty to see that all these are brought to Sri Lanka and distributed to their loved ones. It also enabled us to send items to our loved ones occasionally as we too gave things to be taken to our folk when someone went on vacation.

I made it a point to buy a fairly large refrigerator which was an improvement from the small one we had at home. People were shifting from audio cassettes to audio compact discs during that time and I bought one of them too. I had a full box of fancy items to take home and other valuable things given by everyone around. I did not have enough money in hand as the vacation notice was given so suddenly, but the shops gave me credit and I could manage to buy what I wanted. Most of what we bring back to Sri Lanka came separately by ship. To avoid this everyone hands over their baggage to the shipping company long before they come to Sri Lanka. But this was not possible in my case as I did not get enough notice about my vacation.

The substitute accountant who will carry out my duties during my absence arrived. I had to spend a few days handing over the work to him. He was an Indian national, short and bald headed. He had grown some hair very long in the side of his head which he used to bring to the other side over his scalp to cover his baldness. He took over the work in a few days and now I was ready to come on my vacation. My vacation dates were fixed and my ticket arrived. As I was far away from the International Airport in Riyadh it was necessary to take a domestic flight from the Quisumah airport to Riyadh in order to take a flight to Sri Lanka. The great day came and I was at the airport with bag and baggage to come to Sri Lanka. The Jet which took me from Quisumah to Riyadh was a small one and we felt the jerks very badly. It was Ramadan and fasting time but we were offered refreshments and we consumed them, though the Muslim passengers refrained from consuming anything. The reason we were offered refreshments irrespective of the strict adherence to fasting was because fasting is not applicable to people on a long journey, though I do not know how relevant it is when you travel by jet plane. At the Riyadh airport I had to wait a few hours for the flight to Colombo. I made use of the time to see around the airport just wandering into every nook and corner. Then the magic moment arrived and I was comfortably seated in the Jumbo Jet. It was the same old story travelling by plane. When it touched down in Katunayake, Sri Lanka's international airport, I already felt the fragrance of the greenery and flowers from far far away.

When I came into the airport I felt like being Gulliver in Lilliput. The people looked so small compared to the Arabs and other Middle Eastern nationals whom I saw every day in Saudi Arabia. However it did not take long for me to adapt myself to my homeland. My son was no longer the toddler who crawled on the ground with a limited vocabulary of a few words but was two and a half years and could talk and walk and run. He was now sure that he had a dad and that I was not a mere illusion. However the baby who insisted being in my arms most of the time had got used to being with the mother and came to me only once in a way.

I enjoyed my holiday well. The little extra I earned for over a year was spent during the month for entertainment. Since I always believed in enjoying myself I did not have any reservation in spending what I saved. My brother in law who also worked in a dairy company in Sri Lanka was assigned duties during the same month in the Anuradhapura branch. This gave me the opportunity to join him with my family and visit the ancient cities of Anuradhapura and Pollonnaruwa and take plenty of photographs. I also went to see old friends and attended to distributing the little ornaments which I brought back from the Kingdom.

The holiday month was over in a flash, and towards the end of my holiday I discovered that many of the things I had to do was still in arrears. I was also not well due to the sudden change of climate and the strain of moving about fast to complete all I had to do in one month. On top of it all my luggage which was sent through sea cargo had not arrived in Sri Lanka yet. Taking my sickness as an excuse I managed to get an extension to my vacation by one week. This extra week was enough to do all my unfinished work and to clear the cargo for which I have to be present. Since my vacation time was officially over everyone who would have been expecting parcels from Saudi Arabia would have given up hope thinking I have confiscated the things due to them or that they have got lost in transit. I managed to distribute all the goodies which I brought from Saudi Arabia to the relevant recipients just one day before the date of my flight back to the Kingdom.

Then the day arrived. It was the same routine as I first went to Saudi Arabia. Only difference was that I had experience now and was very much at ease than the first time I left the ground. I made sure that I take everything possible to satisfy my friends in the Kingdom. Local newspapers were much in demand. Then compact discs with local songs were also something they really missed. They missed the local liquor too, but unfortunately there was no way I could help them with that as liquor is taboo in the Kingdom. When I reached the Quisumah Airport all my friends were there to welcome me and I was taken back to the depot in a convoy. Once again I was far away from my loved ones breathing the hot air of the kingdom.

This time things were different from my first arrival. As I had seen my family for a limited time of just over one month, I yearned to see more of them. I was unable to walk into the kitchen because the memory of home cooked meals bothered me. However things went on as usual and I enjoyed life in the best way I can.

As my vacation took more than one year for me to utilize, there was not much time left to complete my two year contract, and before long I got the documents necessary to renew my contract. The new contract was for a higher salary but without overtime. Although in Sri Lanka we will never get overtime as executives, things were different here.

The working hours of the depot was 8 a.m. to 12 noon and 4. p.m. to 8 p.m. Though this was 8 hours of work, it kept you occupied from 8 a.m. to 8 p.m. Some depot accountants overcame this by maintaining a 'that is not my work' attitude or refusing to work beyond working hours, but in my case it was not my style. Our depot was also giving a very good sale with limited resources and therefore the burden on all of us was more. Although you have to sacrifice for the sake of the establishment you work for, it is the duty of the management to see that you are at least partially compensated. But it was not the case here. Your overtime was cut and chopped without any logical reason and without trying to understand the limitations of the depot. On the other hand working without overtime meant that all limitations of the depot will simply go unnoticed with figures and numbers reigning over quality and facilities.

The accommodation of the depot was more or less a tin shed where the poorest of the poor in Sri Lanka live. The reason for this low quality was not because the company did not have resources. It was because the resources went to favoured contractors who did an inferior job and made a fast buck. On the other hand by now I realised that back in Sri Lanka there were about seven people to do the work that I do in the Kingdom. The extra that we earn is just compensation for the extra that we do.

I made a decision regarding my renewal of contract. I declined. On the other hand there were more high paying vacancies available in other companies in the Kingdom itself. The management asked me as to why I do not wish to renew my contract and I gave my reasons. Anyway I had stayed my full two years and was entitled to go home. My son was reaching his school going age and I thought that I have to be there to make sure that he is admitted to the school that I went to. But though I declined to renew my contract I was requested by management to stay on until they could find a replacement for me. This I agreed to as I should not inconvenience the company that I worked for.

Time was now moving fast as I was actually working beyond my contract. After about one month the company sent a replacement for me. I worked with him for a few weeks, but the company was still not able to release me as they needed me in the head office in Riyadh. So after a few weeks of training and transferring the work to the new accountant I moved back to Riyadh.

The Hub of Activity

After spending nearly two years in Hafer Al Batin, I was back in Riyadh and life was a little less boring than it used to be. As the head office was full of people, I could easily mingle with people of all nationalities and it was something I enjoyed. I was accommodated in a room with two other Sri Lankans but was later hijacked with bed and bedding by three Sri Lankan drivers and I had to settle down in their room. I found everyone so friendly and accommodating. Though we shared our meal expenses, I was not allowed to contribute as I was the new arrival or maybe something precious. I overcame this restriction by bringing a few delicacies once in a way and sharing with everyone.

I had very few responsibilities in the head office. The accounting manager had made a new policy of rotating duties so that no one will stagnate in one job. As a result of this I was told to take over from Prudentio the task of collecting data from all over the kingdom and prepare the reports needed by management.

Now I was at the receiving end of the data line. In a depot we prepare the data and transmit them to the head office. So the head office is actually the hub of the wheel. Now I was in most important seat in the company. The work involved interaction with over 20 salesmen compared to just two or three in Hafer Al Batin. But work relating to cash and stocks were nil and that was much less of a headache. I was also able to simplify most of the work that was involved and found myself relaxed and enjoyed whatever free time I had by going into the canteen to dig my teeth into some ice cream.

My routine starts in the morning collecting data from all depots relating to the sales of the previous day. Then I merge them together to prepare the daily sales and the cumulative for the month. One fine day I saw the salesmen thrilled with their figures and planning and aiming high with their monthly commission. When I inquired they told that the sales are extremely high and they are expecting a good return. I just could not see how the sales could shoot up in one day. So when I did some rechecking I found out that the sales for the date have got merged several times. I panicked and managed to prevent the reports from going far. But some copies had already made its way to the sales manager who was also happy about the artificially enhanced figures. It was a big disappointment for everyone once the corrections were done.

I had never experienced MS Windows before. But I saw that all other computers were running on windows except mine. The program for linking and merging sales data was done in dbase 3 plus which is now outdated and the new generation may never have heard of it. So my computer had only DOS which again is now like a horse driven chariot against a Ferrari. The computer screens with Windows were beautiful with the screen looking like a sheet of silk.

I was very good at spreadsheets and Lotus 123 was peanuts to me. Little did I know that my days with Lotus was numbered and I was about to fall in love with the Excel spreadsheet. Mastering it was easy. The help facility embedded in the program was more than enough, and it also had a feature which showed you how to do tasks that you did in Lotus using the commands in Excel. So I was soon an expert in Excel and helped everyone by creating spreadsheets to simplyfy their work.

In the meantime two new accountants arrived from Sri Lanka. They were young and new to the Kingdom, so I was entrusted the task of giving them an orientation of what I was doing. I found it very easy during those days as my workload was eased and the thought that I could leave for home soon made me very happy about their arrival.

Riyadh was much more modern than Hafer Al Batin. Once again I could visit the shopping malls overflowing with gadgets that make you crazy. One fine day when I visited the shopping area I saw the thing I was yearning for. It was a Sony handycam, or in simple terms a small video camera. It was going for a bargain price and I did not hesitate to buy it with whatever savings I had. It was a wonderful investment and was such a novelty. I could not imagine being able to capture everything around you and see it again on a TV without undergoing the pain of developing and printing them at a high cost. Digital cameras were unheard of at that time, and nor were they heard of when I started writing this book. It was said that using a camera in the open was taboo in Saudi Arabia. But sometimes things are exaggerated by those who have stayed longer in the kingdom. The only way to verify this was to be bold and do it to see what happens.

I used my video camera to capture the entire office and factory environment. Even my superiors were interested in this and were demanding copies of my video. I was very happy to give them copies as it gave me a sense of importance.

Time went by and I was longing for the day to go home. With two new accountants I knew it was not far away. Then one fine day the accounting manager approached me and asked whether I could go to Abha for a short period. Abha was an area consisting of mountains and the weather was totally different from most of the kingdom. It was cold throughout the year and there were beautiful parks in every junction. It was also the hot season in the kingdom and everyone was flocking to Abha to enjoy the cool weather and to be away from the heat. I agreed though my return to Sri Lanka was getting delayed. It was also an opportunity and I was always able to see the brighter side of things. The accounting manager told me to stay there and ensure a smooth transition to a new accountant as soon as they send one over to Abha. As it was the season where everyone was travelling to Abha, it was impossible to secure a seat in an aeroplane. So I had to travel by bus. The distance to Ahba from Riyadh was about 1000 kilo metres and it took a little over 10 hours to get there. The bus ride was smooth lasting the entire night and part of the day. Other than some mischievous boys throwing stones at the bus on the way there was nothing interesting and I was asleep through most of the journey.

The bus arrived at Abha and it was not difficult to hire a taxi and find our depot which was very close to a park. There was a big difference in this depot. The depot times were from 8 a.m to 4 p.m. and the manager was very strict with the salesmen and insisted that they should return to the depot before 4 p.m. The salesmen were Sudanese and experienced and I did not need to get involved unnecessarily in their work. The only Sri Lankan in the depot was Peter, the helper in the store, who has been working there for quite a bit of a time.

Though he was a helper he had followed a pharmacist course in Sri Lanka and gave me some support in controlling stocks and maintaining files. This I thought is how an accountant has to work in the depot and the way I worked in Hafer Al Batin was actually far above my job description.

We also had an Indian driver in the depot. Though a driver he was working in the capacity of a salesman doing the related work independently. He was on probation pending a promotion to the level of salesman. I noticed that the drivers from India were very much smarter than our Sri Lankan drivers. They spoke English very fluently and had a broader knowledge of many subjects. One reason was maybe because a person with that much of knowledge will have better employment in Sri Lanka and will not come to Saudi Arabia as a driver.

When there is no pressure of office work Ganesh, the Indian driver would take me to Kamish Musaiyat, a town close to Abha which is more or less a shopping centre visited by all from adjoining towns. The atmosphere was a little liberal in the area and I saw Saudi girls and boys talking to each other in the open though the girls were covered from head to toe. The rules were decided by the 'Muthawas' who were the religious police, and sometimes there could be liberal thinking members among them.

I was someone who had wished to go home to Sri Lanka waiting for a replacement to arrive. So I decided to make the most of my days in the kingdom which were numbered. The Sri Lankan helper had friends around and was with them most of the time. The Indian driver also had Indian friends and they became my friends in no time. As we were away from most of the fun back home we had parties and danced away into the night. Parties coincided with special days back home. As I joined both the Sri Lankans as well as the Indians in whatever they celebrated, I did not forget to record them with my precious possession, the video camera.

An unforgettable event in my stay in Abha was the trip to Al Sooda. Al Sooda was close to Abha and the trip was continuously uphill. Abha was already a hill top, so Al Sooda would have been close to the heavens. Local tourists were arriving from all over to the place. No one sang or danced in the open. Their favourite pastime was to sit around a rug and eat their favourite foods. There was a cable car service at a topmost point in Al Sooda. It was something I did not want to miss. So we bought our tickets and got into one. I felt like a bat hanging on an electric wire. Here we were hanging onto a steel cable by a hook or pulley in a small cabin that kept on going down. In the middle of nowhere the cable car swayed to and fro like a pendulum of a grandfather clock. Yet I knew that these have been moving for a long time without a problem. So I switched on my video camera and aimed it at all the beautiful scenery around me. I had the feeling that photography was considered taboo by most Saudis. So if I asked permission to video a group of Saudis the answer will be a stern 'no'. But I could use my video camera without asking for permission from them. In such an event the Saudis were not responsible for what I did. So I refrained from asking anyone whether to film them, and just kept using my video camera liberally.

The day at Al Sooda was memorable. I did not get such an opportunity in Riyadh or Hafer Al Batin. The time was passing slowly and at last a new accountant came to the depot. After that an orientation went on for some time and I was supposed to come back to Riyadh once he could manage on his own. It was now the end of the tourist season in Abha. Everyone was going back to other towns. It seemed impossible to book a flight back to Riyadh as everyone was leaving Abha. So I decided to come by bus once again. I did not want to take any chances as my stay could get extended due to some new problem.

Back in Riyadh I was preparing to go home. I took count of what I had bought from the kingdom and what was left to buy. I had nothing pending and just the desire to escape the scorching heat and the miserable cold. The greenery, the smiling people and the variety and entertainment also kept me longing to come back to Sri Lanka. The date of departure was fixed and now it was final. At last I breathed a sigh of relief.

Return to Paradise

The journey home was just a routine. Same flight, same work and the same feeling, but happier than before for here I was coming back home for good. The feeling was so enchanting that little did I think of what I was going to do next. But why worry? There was a big demand for accountants, and I will soon be able to establish myself in Sri Lanka.

As my final acquisitions I had a computer which was a Pentium, the fastest in the mid-nineties, and a few other not so important items. I also had some savings which would help me to keep the home fires burning, until I was established. Anyway on top of everything I was now back, at home. Unlike the time I first left Sri Lanka, this time the feeling of being on top of the world came only when the plane touched down. My heart was yearning for home and my belly was looking for the alcohol which was sadly missed in the land where it was taboo.

The journey was smooth. Most of the latter part of the journey in the plane was spent filling up disembarkation forms for many other passengers. Finally we were over Sri Lanka and were landing. I just could not believe it. I was free, no more religious police, no more covered women, no more prayer times and the worst of them all; no more cold weather.

As usual my wife and child were there and so was my dad. We were now coming home. Time passed soon and I had cleared the last bits of my luggage which arrived by sea. However now there was a big question mark. What do I do next?

One by one I began to take account of the new life in Sri Lanka. Unfortunately the initial picture that was bared before me was not at all colourful. My wife has visited an astrologer who had as usual given her some enhanced number about my stay abroad and also advised her on courses of action she has to take. By some unfortunate twist of fate she had got the urge to build a totally unnecessary extra kitchen while the main hall of the house was in a very poor state with broken plaster hanging on the walls. It is sad to note that the additional kitchen was just for 3 people, me, my wife and our only son. In fact she has been suffering most of the time scraping the bottom of all my accounts and spending time looking for building materials. The kitchen was half complete and remained like that and also later served as a hiding place for thieves creeping into our garden.

Then the idea of a motor car had also crept into my wife's mind. Unfortunately the car market at that time was at a peak and buying one meant that you are just looking for a way to dump your money. However the pressure was too much and I said good bye to whatever savings I had with me and brought a heap of iron which moves on 4 wheels and now my wife calmed down. Most of the time I was running around by public transport, looking for spares for the car. Anyway it was a relief. I didn't have to drive it. I had taken the wrong turn already. Now I was rich by a heap of metal and without any of the savings I brought back home.

One major task in my hand was to enrol my son in the same school which I went to. Old students of the school get priority and my son was soon going to the kindergarten of my old school, whose buildings stand so majestically in the heart of the city. Keeping him in the class and leaving was not easy. He still had the fear that someone will suddenly vanish into the sky leaving him behind. In about three days he got used to it and life was ready to move on.

Being back at home did not only mean that I was with my family. I was also close to my friends whom I missed for the past few years. Then when I had free time I visited my friend Siva who lived very close to my own office before I left for Saudi Arabia. When I went there I could not believe my eyes and ears. His real estate agency had flourished and he was minting money. Siva was not the only person who had prospered during my absence. The lady who ran a beauty parlour down the road had her own product now in every supermarket in the country. In fact Sri Lanka had progressed during my absence. . A tuition class, whose teachers used to come to me for computer printouts before I left, has now become a leading computer school. Everyone was talking about email and Internet, though it was not quite broad based. Almost everyone had a mobile phone. In fact technology had progressed at a great pace in Sri Lanka. Here I was just back from the Kingdom with only a few grey hairs as an improvement.

Siva was happy that I was back in Sri Lanka. He offered me work in his business as he could do with a sidekick at least till I found employment. It was most welcome and working with Siva was fun. However I kept applying for jobs in the weekend papers as I had to get established as an Accountant soon.

In most of the interviews I attended I got short listed to about four candidates. But being the best was not always easy. Then I got selected for a job in a garment buying office in Colombo which owned two factories in the hill capitol where the weather was cold. I was promised a good salary and a car once the profits start coming in. However soon I discovered that the chairman had no talent in business and had a long line of creditors behind him and a long history of ruining businesses.

Though the company had no money to buy tea and sugar, it would run a colourful advertisement in the weekend newspapers once in a way calling for applications for new vacancies. Such an advertisement would read as follows:

Vacancies exist for energetic individuals as accountants, marketing executives, production managers, trainees etc. If you are looking for a healthy work environment and a salary above market rates please send your resume along with copies of certificates and testimonials. Successful candidates must be willing to travel abroad periodically, at short notice.

The advertisement was just a booster to maintain the corporate image and to hoodwink whoever is stupid enough to deal with the company. However applications come in thousands, the paper can be sold to the hardware to supplement the company income. All those people who have taken pains to prepare their applications, take photocopies and send them have been taken for a ride. The advertisement reminds me of a story where a city was surrounded by enemy soldiers with the intention of starving everyone in the town to death. When the food was over and they had only one loaf of bread left for the entire town, one wise man threw it at the enemies outside saying that they have plenty and would like to share. The enemies seeing that the town had enough food to throw away left the siege thinking that they will die of starvation first.

The most dreaded day at work was pay day. We were dumped in the factories without enough money to pay the salaries and the chairman would bolt form the scene leaving us to face the music. Looking at all the faces who were smiling when our vehicle arrived suddenly go pale when the full salary cannot be paid made me nearly sick. Things were not in my favour with most of the time explaining to the bank managers that one day we will be covered with gold when I knew things are actually going from bad to worse. The chairman got over his cash problem by falling out with his staff. When the staff was leaving one by one, I began my routine of applying for jobs again. Before long I was called for an interview in a place little far away from Colombo. It looked as if I was selected already and that they were waiting for me to come to the interview. Anyway here I was starting work in the second company after my arrival in Sri Lanka.

Going back to my previous workplace I came to know that the chairman has had other motives in recruiting me. As I was back from the Middle East he would have expected me to have enough money to provide capital to his business. However I did not have money to part with. I would also not have parted with it even if I had, and the plan never materialized. The next accountant who joined the company was not so lucky, and he had fallen prey to this plan. I met him in the Tax Department and when he told me about what happened, I just asked him how he, as an accountant could not see that the business was not viable and was moving towards disaster.

The Man of Steel

My childhood hero was Superman, also well known as the man of steel. In no way did I anticipate that one fine day in my career I will meet him in person. This particular person I am about to refer to had many things in common with the comic book hero. He had X-ray vision, he could travel at the speed of light, he could hover above the ground and most of all he could bend steel with such grace.

This was how I would describe the owner of the new company I joined. He had started very small and had now come to a turning point in the business. The main business of the organization was steel furniture. As of today it has branches all over the country and beyond. However from my experience in life I now know that this is not an achievement that is impossible for others. Some businesses fail and some make it right to the top. Many people treat their initial failures as a bad sign or signal to stop proceeding further. They blame it on their stars, the weather, the rulers or their wife. It is the few who brave the initial repetitive failures who make it to the top.

I once knew a person who was an expert repairing vehicle bodies. His work was neat and in demand. He worked under contract to a garage and would repair car bodies as a sub-contractor to the garage. All he had to do was to visit the garage when he was called and do a repair and all materials and equipment was supplied by the garage. However for 2 days work, the garage would charge Rs.12,000 from the customer and give this person only Rs.4,000. He was constantly lamenting about the sum the garage is getting though an amount of Rs.4,000 for 2 days was a fortune. So he could not continue the venture for long. However if he was the garage owner he would definitely be lamenting about the Rs.4,000 that he has to give a sub-contractor. This nature prevented him from getting anywhere to the top.

Coming back to steel bending there were enough computers in the company to go around. Something that was not very common before I left for Saudi Arabia. Most of its activities were computerized. However though the accounting function was also computerised they did not even have a trial balance which balanced. Those in the accountancy profession will know the importance of the accuracy of the trial balance, and when done with the computer it cannot be wrong at least arithmetically. However this was a unique situation altogether. The computer programmer though smart did not have an accounting background. But he did his part well. The programme was based on the DOS (Disk Operated Systems) based software and I was able to dive into it and take a look to see what's happening. It was a challenge for me. The accounting program was based on Foxbase, could be compared to MSAccess that is common today. The programmer had not created a user friendly program. Instead he got involved with it most of the time, cutting and chopping to correct figures when the need arose, without giving any respect to the double entry system, which is the base of all controls in accounting. Before long I discovered the root of the problem. My next step was to ensure that the future Trial Balance of the organization was arithmetically accurate. It was also achieved and things were now smooth. The CEO was so happy that my salary was retroactively increased and I was promised a vehicle in a few months although I never asked for one.

Before the trial balance the Man of Steel had his own way of monitoring his business. He had selected a particular day of the month on which he takes stock of everything in his business. He would do this without fail on the same day every month. This would also include assets like debtors, bank balances etc., which can be extracted from the books. He will also take the liabilities and subtract it from the total assets that he worked out. Then he would see by how much his net asset value has changed from the previous month. According to him if the net asset value has increased his business is improving taking into consideration everything including theft, waste and his upkeep. What he prepares monthly is of course the "Statement of Affairs" in accounting terminology. However this is the first time I saw someone making good use of this principle, even when the accounting system was in chaos.

We were operating in the head office which was far away from the capital city of Colombo. The building was still under construction and we were working in the ground floor, with 3 more stories yet to come up. A little away from this location was the factory spanning a large area with the house of the CEO right in the middle like the fortress of a king surrounded by his army. Yet the company was still in its developing stage with just one small showroom in Colombo, almost invisible to passers' by.

The man of Steel naturally had an iron hand. It came down hard on those that do not fit in. The attendance register was available only till opening time. It will be locked away on the dot, and was replaced by a late attendance register. This late attendance register had just 4 cages per employee per month. After using these four cages on four days he had no place to sign and was considered to be on no pay leave. Being an executive I was exempt from this rule, but yet late arrival affected the annual bonus.

The strict rules in force could be one of the reasons for the business' success, but not the main reason. It was sheer ability and dedication. The products which were manufactured had a very economical relationship with each other. Off cuts from foam mattresses will be bonded together as cushions for chairs. It was the same with plywood remaining after making a door. When a product was in its initial stages he would not hesitate to get everyone's opinion on the finished item. Yet it was him alone who finally made the decision, and he would take that responsibility upon himself.

As promised soon I was given a new van imported just for me, and that was a turning point in my career with the Iron Company. The company was improving fast and the present characteristics soon had to change. The building was still being built. The trademark looked a little lousy. The letterhead was a small piece of paper which was not too small to qualify as a small sticky note. However big changes were around the corner.

As a first step a showroom was planned very close to Colombo, Sri Lanka's commercial capital. A large building was rented out renovated and modified and it was ready with the goods in no time. Now we needed salesman. At that time the company was still in its infancy that it was very difficult to find salesmen fluent in English even after a newspaper advertisement in the best-selling week end newspaper. I too was in the interview panel and managed to find just too candidates who could manage their English, and one of them was very fluent and confident in his conversation. Naturally those two were selected. One of them was assigned to the new showroom in the city.

Next was the sales promotion part. An advertising agency was given the task of placing a full page advertisement which will cost a fortune in almost all the Sunday newspapers. When the prepared advertisement was brought, the owner's uncle who was an English teacher as I remember was critical of the paragraph describing a large chair which adorned the entire page.

This is how it went as far as I can remember:

"The above chair is manufactured to international standards AND it has undergone all tests of quality AND it is ideal for your office AND not only will you like it but also the whole staff."

Though I tried to remember the paragraph that was seen nearly 20 years ago I know that the last part after the AND is fully accurate. The owners uncle had pointed out that it was grammatically incorrect and written his own using all rules of English grammar but was not pleasing to the reader. On comparing these two I pointed out that the advertising company has used a poetic and pleasing way to attract the reader and it need not be grammatically correct. Though the owner was still not convinced I suddenly noticed something very interesting in the paragraph. It was the sentence after the last AND. "not only will you like it but also the whole staff"

I asked the owner whether he found something special in this sentence. He did not notice. I asked him what it means. He said that because the chair looks nice He and the whole staff are going to like it. Then I asked him whether it does not mean that he will like it and start using it, and being happy will also have a special liking towards the staff. He thought for a moment and realised the attraction of the sentence. No, "Da Vinci Code" was not available at that time. The advertisement appeared just as it was planned by the advertising company and was a new beginning.

The owner of the company was mostly concentrating on his income. He did not have any reservations about giving more to the staff. In fact he was very generous to the staff. However the staff had to survive first. Actually he had an iron fist over everything. He did not tolerate the slighted mistake and punishment was always in cash and a verbal onslaught. It was so effective that very few came for work after a mistake. He also expected the staff to move along with him. But it was impossible to keep pace with him. Those who lagged behind were soon left behind as they could not cope with the speed.

I soon experienced this myself. I was promoted to the post of General Manager maybe as an appreciation for my contribution to their accounts. However this was just an icon for my fluency in English. The General Manger was made a Director of the company to pave the way for my promotion. I was never a good administrator but I was not required to administer. But now the company had a good accounting system and the future looked very bright. Suddenly the new van given to me was taken back and replaced with an older one which was still quite good. When that too was taken away and common transport was provided, I once again began to apply for new jobs. While going for interviews I also gave my resignation, giving adequate time to finalize things before leaving. As of today even the General Manager who was made a Director has also left the company, just like many of the other employees.

Business for dummies

I was never scared to walk out of a job. There was plenty of work to do by way of freelance consultancy. Above all I knew that Siva the real estate agent would always make more money with me as a sidekick. So there I was again walking to Sivas den free as a bird and relaxed like a kitten. No more tension or fixed working hours.

I did not have any problem with earning as I would earn the same amount that I would have received as a salary from a company. The day was spent going about in my almost vintage vehicle, for which I was also paid. Life was smooth but yet I had to find employment and save my "Accountant" tag. So I did not stop applying for jobs. Then one day a friend called me and told about a vacancy in a company. He also said that the company was in a financial crisis, and my job was to resurrect it from its near death. I was scared after my garment company experience but my friend convinced me that the owners are good people and will reward me if I perform.

An interview was arranged and I met the chairman in his residence. It was then that I came to know that he was also a qualified cost accountant with much more experience than me. "How could things go wrong?" I thought. He did not mention about a crisis but admitted that things are not going well. He said that they have a clear mark up of 85% on the products and that something is radically wrong. By the way the company was producing polythene products for the export market. I was impressed by his attitude, but yet having a few bad experiences in my previous jobs was still a bit paranoid about the whole set up. For instance I already had a bad experience with a company without any money, who could not pay salaries on time.

However I was willing to take up the job. There was one question I posed to the chairman. I asked him what will happen if the company comes out of whatever financial crisis it is in. Will my services not be needed and won't I get redundant after that. He did not agree, he told that once things are bright we can think of diversification, opening new businesses and much more. I was impressed. I gave my consent to join the company. He said he will let me know about his decision and later gave me a date to start work. The factory was again far from the city but not as far as the steel company. The product being polythene was also not as hard as the product of the steel company.

The day I started work the administration manager took me around and introduced me to the staff. Just one of them was known to me previously, but the others were also friendly and all smiles. Then he sat down for a discussion with me. He explained to me about the profit margin they have on their products and that the profit is tied somewhere. The question is "Where?" However I was not at all convinced. I told him that I can smell a great crisis when I looked around. I noticed that the whole place was engulfed by an eerie gloom. The shining look of prosperity was nowhere to be seen. But my job was to correct it and to bring sunshine to the place.

I sat with ease in spite of the fear of doubt burning in me. I checked the sales invoices and purchase orders and was satisfied that goods were priced with a mark-up of over 85 per cent. But there was something hidden somewhere. It could be pilferage, theft, a miscalculation and many other things. The accounts were of course in chaos. Final statements were in arrears for so many years. Electricity bills were not paid up to the tune of millions. Money was owed to customs for duty on clearance of goods. In fact everyone was trembling when the phone rang. It was always someone to whom the company owes money.

However the most fascinating thing was the refunds receivable on Value Added Tax. The company was approved under export incentives and whatever VAT that was paid was refundable after submitting of returns. The company though in a crisis had not filed these returns and was yet to receive a refund of Rs.2,000,000 which was enough money for two containers of raw material. On the other hand the company had to pay penalties of Rs.900,000 for non-submission of VAT returns. Before analysing the crisis of the company, here I found money to be taken quickly and worked on it. I managed to bring in Rs.1,100,000 which was the amount receivable less the penalty payable. My first task was this and it was a boost to a cash starved organization. Then I kept working on it while also attending to other work and reduced the penalty of Rs.900,000 to Rs.11,000 bringing another amount over Rs.800,000.

The former paragraph would have been more than enough to understand the inefficiency that has led this company into chaos. But that was just the tip of the iceberg. I wanted to know how the operations of the company were doing and took a few shipments in order to calculate the profit. However I ended up with staggering loss figures and showed them to the chairman. The chairman was not convinced. He believed that it could not be. On further investigation I found where things have gone wrong.

Polythene is mainly made form a few materials known as "Poly Ethylene". The final product was priced based on the input of these materials. It also used colouring known as "Master Batch" which is used in quantities as small as 3 per cent or 5 per cent and was ignored. However this was expensive and cost about six to eight times the cost of Poly Ethylene. Eureka, so there it is. Though the quantity is small price-vice it could be as high as 40% of the cost. Though the horse was nowhere to be seen it was still not too late to close the stable door and bring in a new horse. So the costing was put on track, but what do we do about the accumulated losses?

The next thing that I was suspecting was pilferage. But there should be a system to control usage of material and a measurement to see whether it has gone into the product. There was a wonderful and complex system to control costs. It was a well-designed form showing the material usage, the absorption of costs, giving exact percentages used and the final profit. It was so advanced and complex that it did not work. My first decision was to simplify this control procedure. Why do we have to create complex forms for a product that mainly uses just 4 types of raw material that come in large bags? I designed 4 stock cards which give the issue and usage of these materials in units of bags, which made measurement easy. For the master batch which is used in small quantities separate cards were designed to record usage in grams.

There was some resistance from the factory floor. Some came out with the problem that will arise when a full bag is not emptied into the extruder machine. I told them to include it as half a bag. Then they told it may not be exactly half a bag. Then I said just guess how much of a bag it is, but make sure that the balance when put into another job is recorded properly. Finally the control system was implemented. It was impossible to cheat on this document. If 100 bags were issued to the factory, the 4 stock cards had to reflect the amount of bags issued to the machines, giving the remaining number of bags on the factory floor.

These stock cards enabled us to calculate the cost of material that goes into a job, and compare it with the sale price. If the material was stolen, we will not arrive at the usual margin. We could also decide whether a job should continue and monitor jobs that made a loss. There was much resistance but it was a success.

We were able to ensure that the company no longer produced anything at a direct loss. However we had to deal with the losses that were accumulated. The company was initially funded by its offshore partner and millions of dollars have been provided as soft loans. However, all these funds have been completely exhausted without any benefit to the organisation. However the loans still remain to be paid. In addition to this dollar loans have been obtained from a local bank, and that too had to be repaid with interest.

We did a simple plan for the future. First of all we calculated the total monthly commitment including the past losses that are to be paid during any particular month. Whatever the amount was, polythene was also a very profitable business. We discovered that the sale after converting just 4 containers of raw material into a product with the least profit margin is more than enough to keep the office on track. Everyone accepted this. But did not have the discipline to stick to it. The formula is simple. If a shop earns an income of 200 dollars per month before payment of rent and the rent is 201 dollars per month, the business will accumulate a loss of one dollar a month until all its resources are depleted. Therefore the shop has to maintain an income about 202 if it is to progress and develop.

There were too many decision makers in the company, yet no one to take the blame for any decision. Even when the opportunity was there the 4 container formula was upset by postponing production to the following month because the margin was high. Unfortunately the simple arithmetic of profit was suppressed by a more complex unprofitable calculation. Anyway this did not stop me from bringing about order to the organization.

After some time even though at a slow pace, the company began to show improvement. However I could notice the foxes and rabbits theory which I saw in a very old computer program taking shape. The program involves an island of foxes and rabbits. The foxes live by eating rabbits. Therefore the fox population increases when there are many rabbits. However the more the foxes the more the rabbits are consumed, and the rabbit population declines rapidly. With no rabbits for food, the foxes die of starvation, and the fox population declines. With no foxes to eat them, the rabbit population begins to increase. Then once again there is food for the foxes. In this company the operation was ruined by decision making foxes. Once the resources were depleted these foxes too had gone into hibernation. However when things were improving we could see the foxes coming out from their burrows.

Being a company with special approval from the Board of Investment of Sri Lanka, it was exempt from customs duty and income tax. However they have to ensure that all products manufactured are exported. The company was allowed a small percentage of local sales, yet customs duty had to be paid for such sales. However there were a lot of underhand dealings in this area. Most of the work done were ones carried out by some of the factory staff for their own benefit. It was not possible to monitor this as it brought in a small profit to the company.

The chairman of the company had the habit of making sudden and quick decisions. Unfortunately everyone agrees with them and some maintain a neutral stand. I was the only one who opposed them if they appeared to be wrong according to my knowledge. However most of the time wrong decisions were the ones that were finally implemented.

The company had permission to sell a stipulated percentage in the local market, after paying customs duty. This fact could have been easily exploited simply by making a few book entries. The chairman could have registered a new company to sell polythene products locally, and the main company could sell its legal percentage to it at a very small profit margin. The second company could sell it locally and earn a wonderful profit. However the chairman's decision was to remove some machines and to relocate them somewhere else. The machines were large and consumed lot of electricity. As usual everyone lauded it as a great idea. I tried with all my energy to convince the chairman not to do it but a few simple journal entries will do the job. However going by head count he went ahead with the plan.

After the machines were relocated we came to know that some of them had a relationship with other machines in the production cycle. A lot of inconvenience was caused and as usual it was a flop.

With whatever setbacks we had to face I was convinced that still there is a light at the end of the tunnel. Things had anyway changed from what it was when I joined the place. The staff was no longer suffering from telephone phobia as most of our creditors were being paid. Even the bank gave temporary overdrafts in time of need. There were no electricity bills or customs duties in arrears. There was also a lot of room for improvement. However the staff has got used to a particular pattern and the strength of the staff was not sufficient to make a significant change in the organization. I wanted to recruit more staff but we also had to consider our financial constraints. When I explored the options available to us I found that a government organization named "Dawn of Youth" provided qualified university graduates to companies and even paid them the salary for a number of months. The terms were very attractive. We need not pay them anything and also are not under obligation to employ them after the initial period.

I got permission from the chairman and employed three girls who were really smart and had great hope to put the company on full gear. In addition to the salary provided by "Dawn of Youth" we too gave them an additional 10 dollars just to maintain our dignity. I was very happy that I had a strong team with me to develop the company and mainly to fight the corruption that was eating into the company's profits.

However little did I realise that there was a conspiracy hatching and there was a need to get rid of them by those who were affected by their enthusiasm. Unfortunately evil wins and when they refused to help in the factory due to a bottleneck which was again a result of inefficiency, those who did not want the new staff around were able to convince the chairman to sack them and he has made the decision to do so while I was not present. At this point I knew that the organisation cannot be developed and began to apply for new jobs.

To see the sea

While continuing my work with the plastic people I faced many interviews and got short listed in many. Finally I was selected for a job in a fisheries company far from Colombo but close to where I live. It was time to leave the polythene company and taking over at the fishery was smooth. I was introduced to everyone by another accountant in charge of an associate company and the directors were also very nice people. Another important character was the general manager who was also a qualified accountant. He was dedicated and hardworking and would have been the mastermind behind the company's success.

Another character of interest was my secretary and everyone was calling her "honey". I felt odd to call her like that and inquired about her name. She was Malay and her name was actually "Honi Nizam". Thank God it was not pronounced "horny". So everyone was actually calling her name. I too called her that way, it was not difficult as I was used to calling girls by their pet names.

Honi was a sensitive character, and I was told she was inefficient. However from my past experience I knew I could train anybody and get them to work. Thus I began work in a very pleasant environment.

The company's activity was only fishing and exporting the fish. They had two large trawlers for fishing in the sea and they also had Thai fishermen with their own boats doing sub contracts for them.

Their main catch was Tuna and Marlin. One fish is definitely over 25 kgs and sometimes went up to 100 kgs. The process involved was the same for all shipments. Fish were unloaded at the fisheries harbour and cleaning took place immediately. This was packed in boxes with dry ice, and were immediately taken to the airport for export. The company had a bunch of efficient and dedicated people who were able to produce results. The company also had plenty of cash resources and after my previous experiences with bankrupt companies the touch of money was soothing to the fingers.

The work was mainly a little bit of administration, the daily routine payments, tax matters and final accounts. In addition to this each shipment was separately assessed and there was no possibility of things going in the wrong direction.

My secretary, Honi was pretty ad boisterous. She made it a point to remain pretty and had an occasional tiff with one or more of her colleagues. However these fights did not last long and added to the fun of office life.

Honi showed great potential, but was not without a few errors here and there. One area where errors occurred was in writing cheques. We all know that cheques need to be 100% accurate for the bank to honour them. However sometimes it is easy to do the work than to correct someone else's mistake. For example when one letter in a sentence is missing as a habit, there is a high probability that we too will overlook this. Therefore it is easier to write it ourselves. But this would increase my work and reduce the work of my secretary. I did not want such a situation to arise. I put my mind to work and ended up developing and excel worksheet to print cheques accurately. It became very popular with the directors and we said good bye to manual cheque writing.

Things were happening rather fast and everyone was running about doing their work. The general manager was putting 100% into the company. He would be there when fish is being cut as well as when vehicles were reversed. I also noticed that he was not very keen on delegating and creating a second level of managers so that he could relax a little bit. However from my past experiences I have learnt that this attitude is correct. It is sometimes necessary to maintain your value and create a situation where you are indispensable.

One fine day I was going through the personal files of some Thai nationals and saw a new name called "Pen Ding". I was unable to find any documents relating to him such as passport, visa etc. After a painful search I discovered that it was the file of "pending" documents and Honi had broken the word and written it as Pen Ding. In another instance I was trying to locate a ship whose name was written illegibly. Finally I discovered that it was the word "workmanship".

The company was still using a manual system of accounting. However the directors felt the need for a computer system and we migrated to it successfully. Work was smooth and the money kept coming in and this was very pleasant.

The operations of the company was actually a temporary one which kept on getting renewed. One fine day when the general manager informed me that the operation may not continue beyond a certain month I began to apply for jobs again.

Response to applications were very good and prompt and I was called to take up work in a car spare part manufacturing company. The accountant who was already employed was leaving to a place close to his home as he was travelling from far away. However after I took over the other accountant's job got cancelled and he was unable to leave. In order not to create an embarrassing situation I decided to leave.

Back to the future

As usual I went to meet Siva, my stop gap between employments. He was as usual happy as he was inundated with work and immediately suggested that we first go to the hill capital to relax and come back to start work.

While we were far from the city I got one invitation for an urgent interview which I missed due to our trip, but I did not regret it and do not regret it today. We worked together as in the past and my income was decent enough and much more than when being employed.

At this point nearly ten years ago when I looked back at my career and was simply astonished to see the number of people I worked for. It was such that some interviewers suspect that I will not stay with them very long. I had a clear idea of how people succeed and how they fail and how they play the blame game when they fail.

For instance I know that the plastic company made great progress after I joined them and collapsed after I left. Today it is no more and has closed down. But if anyone inquires about my contribution they will say that due to external conditions things improved and due to the same reason things went wrong after I left. When it comes to the steel company my contribution was minute and whatever progress it made is due to the mastermind of the chairman. But he still mentions how my contribution to its accounts put the company on top gear.

While working for Siva I also received a call form a cousin of mine to help him with his accounts as he has opened an office to sell motor vehicles to clients who needed them. He earned a very good income but was also a spendthrift which kept his company from developing further. But it was enough to keep things going. I also launched a website for his car sale which would have been one of the first such sites in Sri Lanka. However he did not make much use of it. Charging small sums from clients to advertise was of no use to him when he was now selling them with a high mark up.

Things were going on well with myself working for Siva and occasionally for my cousin. During this time my wife's old house was torn down and a new one was built which was in the Colombo city and we moved into this house.

A few days after we moved into this house it was chaos again. Sri Lanka was hit by a devastating tsunami just after Christmas day in 2004. The experience was new to the country and only a few including myself knew that it was called a "tsunami". People were totally unaware that they mowed into the sea when the water receded exposing more the beach. However the waves came back with such force that even railway engines drifted like matchboxes.

The world is full of sympathy and the donations were pouring into the country and many non-profit making organization were active in voluntary work after the aftermath. It was then that Siva was approached by an administrator regarding a vacancy in the Tsunami Finance Unit of his organization. He knew Siva as he has recommended accommodation to him and knew Siva will find the right person, and that is exactly what Siva did.

This was in 2005 and here I am still working for them with a few years more for retirement. Everyone who knows my work history ask whether I am still working in the same place. Right now life is peaceful there are no bombs exploding around the country as the war with the Tamil Tigers were over. It is the time for me to end my book as I do not wish to continue my story to my present workplace. So for the time being "Chaos Unlimited" has ended.

www.ingramcontent.com/pod-product-compliance
Lightning Source LLC
Chambersburg PA
CBHW061445180526
45170CB00004B/1563